'MURDER WILL OUT'

'MURDER WILL OUT'

The Detective in Fiction

T. J. BINYON

Oxford   New York
OXFORD UNIVERSITY PRESS
1989

Oxford University Press, Walton Street, Oxford OX2 6DP
Oxford New York Toronto
Delhi Bombay Calcutta Madras Karachi
Petaling Jaya Singapore Hong Kong Tokyo
Nairobi Dar es Salaam Cape Town
Melbourne Auckland
and associated companies in
Berlin Ibadan

Oxford is a trade mark of Oxford University Press

British Library Cataloguing in Publication Data
Binyon, T. J.
The detective in fiction
1. Detective fiction in English to 1985 - Critical
Studies
I. Title
823'.0872
ISBN 0-19-219223-X

Library of Congress Cataloging in Publication Data
Binyon, T. J.
Murder will out / T. J. Binyon.
p. cm.
1. Detective and mystery stories, American—History and criticism.
2. Detective and mystery stories, English—History and criticism.
3. Detective in literature. I. Title
PS374.D4B56 1989 813'.0872'09—dc19 88-37115
ISBN 0-19-219223-X

Typeset by Colset Private Limited, Singapore
Printed in Great Britain
by Biddles Ltd.
Guildford & King's Lynn

To my Mother

Detective story: one in which a detective or detectives solve the crime.

Ordean A. Hagen, *Who Done It?*

CONTENTS

Note

The titles quoted in the text are, unless it is stated otherwise, those in
which the detective in question first appears.

Chapter 1

IN THE BEGINNING: DUPIN AND LECOQ

'You remind me of Edgar Allan Poe's Dupin. I had no idea that such individuals did exist outside of stories.'

Sherlock Holmes rose and lit his pipe. 'No doubt you think that you are complimenting me in comparing me to Dupin,' he observed. 'Now, in my opinion, Dupin was a very inferior fellow. . . .'

'Have you read Gaboriau's works?' I asked. 'Does Lecoq come up to your idea of a detective?'

Sherlock Holmes sniffed sardonically. 'Lecoq was a miserable blunderer,' he said, in an angry voice.

(A. Conan Doyle, *A Study in Scarlet*)

The following pages are an attempt at a history not of a type of fiction, but of a type of fictional character: the central figure, the protagonist, of the detective story or crime novel, the fictional detective in all his guises, ranging from brilliant, eccentric amateur to plodding, imperceptive policeman. Such an approach might appear distinctly odd in dealing with any other type of fiction. Here it is legitimized not only because, uniquely, the genre grew out of the character, rather than vice versa, but also because, again uniquely, the character has so often overshadowed and become detached from the author. More people know of Sherlock Holmes and Hercule Poirot than of Conan Doyle and Agatha Christie.

In 1928, at the height of the golden age of the detective story, Dorothy L. Sayers, one of the most popular detective story writers of the time, put together an anthology of short stories entitled *Great Short Stories of Detection, Mystery and Horror*. The first two stories in the detection section, 'The History of Bel' and 'The History of Susanna', were taken from the Apocrypha; the third, 'The Story of Hercules and Cacus', from Virgil's *Aeneid*, Book VIII, and the fourth, 'The Story of Rhampsinitus', from Herodotus, Book II. In the introduction to the volume, a brilliant short history of the crime story containing fascinating observations on technique and method of narration, Sayers remarks that the detective story 'possesses an Aristotelian perfection of beginning, middle and end'. Later, in an essay entitled 'Aristotle on Detective Fiction' printed in her book *Unpopular Opinions* (1946), she expanded on this remark, maintaining—if with her tongue in her cheek—that the whole of Aristotle's *Poetics* was written with the detective story in mind.

This insistence on the ancient lineage of the genre, combined with the attempt to link it with the founding father of literary theory, constitutes an obvious attempt to establish its intellectual respectability and to defend it against the accusation often levelled that it is cheap, sensational trash with no literary value whatsoever. Much quoted and much anthologized in this context is the chapter from Voltaire's *Zadig* (1747) entitled 'Le Chien et le Cheval', in which the eponymous hero deduces the appearance of the Queen of Babylon's dog and the King of Babylon's horse from the traces they have left behind them. The story appears to prove not only that the detective story is older, and hence more respectable, than is generally believed, but also that great authors were not above employing its methods.

The example is not altogether successful, for Voltaire, of course, is not interested in the anecdote as an example of the science of deduction, but rather as one more demonstration of the miserable plight of the rational being in a society composed primarily of unreasoning ones. Nor, indeed, is it really Voltaire's story: he did not bother to invent it, but adapted it from an episode in the Chevalier de Mailly's *Les Voyages et les aventures des trois princes de Serendip*, published in Paris in 1719. Here the three princes, like Zadig, demonstrate their powers of deduction by describing a camel, its load, and its rider without having seen any of them.

Though Voltaire's use of the story might have been perverse, the anecdote itself could perhaps be seen as the archetypal example of the deductive method, since it appears in so many forms in so many literatures. Mailly's book was not original either; it was an unacknowledged translation of Christoforo Armeno's *Peregrinaggio di tre giovani figliuoli del Re di Serendippo* (Venice, 1557), which itself claimed to be a translation of a Persian original. In fact, it appears to be the fusion into a single narrative of a number of Persian stories and motifs, while the anecdote demonstrating the powers of observation and deduction of a young man or young men is to be found not only in Persian, but also in Arabic, Turkish, Indian, and Hebrew folk-tales. Other authors who have employed the story since then include Alexandre Dumas, who gives an adaptation of it in a chapter of *Le Vicomte de Bragelonne* (1848); there, d'Artagnan, by observing the traces left behind by an affray in a wood, is able to tell Louis XIV what has happened there. Most recently it has appeared, in a version which keeps very close to Voltaire, in the opening pages of Umberto Eco's medieval detective story *Il nome della rosa* (1980; translated into English as *The Name of the Rose*, 1983). Although Brother William of Baskerville has not seen the abbot's lost horse, he is able, on meeting the servants sent out to look for it, to describe it minutely and even to name it.

Voltaire is not the only eighteenth-century writer to be seen as a precursor of the modern detective novelist; Defoe, author of *Robinson Crusoe* (1719), has also been put forward, not so much because he displays an interest in deduction, but because his works so often take crime and the criminal as their subject: either real, as in *The History of the Remarkable Life of John Sheppard* (1724) and *The Life of Jonathan Wild* (1725), or fictional, as in the novels *Moll Flanders* (1722) and *Roxana* (1724). And at the end of the century the political philosopher William Godwin, whose daughter was to marry Shelley and whose stepdaughter was to bear a child to Byron, composed *The Adventures of Caleb Williams* (1794), often cited as the first true crime novel. Certainly a bald résumé of the plot supports this view: the eponymous hero-cum-narrator suspects that his employer, Falkland, has committed a murder and has fastened suspicion for the crime on a father and son who have been executed. Fearing what Williams might uncover, Falkland fires him, frames him for theft, and relentlessly persecutes him. But at the end of the novel Williams publicly accuses Falkland of murder, whereupon the latter confesses and dies. However, Godwin's interests, like Voltaire's, do not lie in crime and detection; rather, his aim was to show 'the tyranny and perfidiousness exercised by the powerful members of the community against those who are less privileged than themselves'; and in the original version Falkland, when accused, maintains his innocence, and Williams, half mad, goes to prison.

In the search for illustrious sponsors historians of the detective story have not ignored Dickens, whose Inspector Bucket in *Bleak House* (1852–3) is often referred to as the first police detective in English fiction. Dickens based the character on a real police-officer, Inspector Charles Field, about whom he had written in the magazine *Household Words* in 1850. In *The Moonstone* (1868) Wilkie Collins,

Dickens's friend and contemporary, also used a real figure—Sergeant Whicher, famous for his work on the so-called 'Road Murder' of 1860—as the model for his police-officer, Sergeant Cuff, who is called in to investigate the loss of the famous diamond. Cuff plays a much more important part in the novel than does Bucket in *Bleak House*. Indeed, no less a critic than T. S. Eliot has written, in 'Wilkie Collins and Dickens' (1927), that *The Moonstone* is 'the first and greatest of English detective novels', a judgement which historians delight in quoting, for obvious reasons, despite its depressing implications for the contemporary writer.

Later in the same essay Eliot makes a comparison between the English detective story, in which the human element is said to predominate and which he sees as deriving from Collins, and the 'pure' detective story, 'something as specialized and as intellectual as a chess problem', which has its origin in the stories of Edgar Allan Poe (1809–49). The argument is difficult to sustain, and, more than that, with the mention of Poe the game is up: the first proper fictional detective and the first proper detective stories have been discovered. The attempt to trace the genre back to the beginning of time is impossible; although, as we have seen, isolated, discrete elements of subject and narration may easily be found, they do not add up to a whole. Unlike almost any other literary genre, the detective story owes its origin to one author alone. And if one cannot go all the way with the American critic Philip Van Doren Stern, who has written 'Like printing, the detective story has been improved upon only in a mechanical way since it was first invented; as artistic products, Gutenberg's Bible and Poe's "The Murders in the Rue Morgue" have never been surpassed', certainly Poe's detective stories remain the only ones to have been written by a literary genius. Symptomatic of the power of Poe's influence on later authors is the pseudonym adopted by one of Japan's better-known detective story writers, Hirai Taro (b. 1894), who called himself Edogawa Rampo (pronounced 'Edoga-aram-po'). It seems doubtful, however, that the methods of Taro's detective, who in one story disguises himself as an overstuffed armchair, would have been countenanced by Dupin (*Japanese Tales of Mystery and Imagination*, 1956).

Of course, Poe had no intention of writing detective stories or of creating a detective. His central figure, the Chevalier C. Auguste Dupin, with his predilection for a nocturnal existence, who chooses for his residence 'a time-eaten and grotesque mansion, long deserted through superstitions . . . and tottering to its fall in a retired and desolate portion of the Faubourg St. Germain', is recognizably kin to the narrators of other stories such as 'Ligeia' (1838) or 'The Fall of the House of Usher' (1839). And the ratiocinative urge displayed by Dupin in his investigation of crime is earlier to be found, for example, in the essay 'Maelzel's Chess-Player' (1836), in which the author endeavours to discover, through a succession of logical inferences, the secret of a famous chess-playing automaton.

In Dupin Poe created the prototype of the great detective, the eccentric genius with stupendous reasoning powers, whose brilliance is given added refulgence by the fact that he is always accompanied and his investigative *tours de force* always set down by a loyal, admiring, but uncomprehending and imperceptive friend and assistant. Though primordial, Poe's stories are far from primitive. In the stories in which Dupin plays a part—'The Murders in the Rue Morgue' (1841), 'The Mystery of Marie Rogêt' (1842) and 'The Purloined Letter' (1845)—and in two others—'The Gold-Bug' (1843) and 'Thou Art the Man' (1844)—Poe adumbrates many of the themes and devices of later writers. The most obvious are the locked-room mystery ('The Murders in the Rue Morgue'), the technique of abstract deduction from reported facts ('The Mystery of Marie Rogêt'), the art of concealment by display ('The Purloined Letter'), and the scientific method of deciphering coded messages ('The Gold-Bug'). And 'Thou Art the Man' provides us with the least likely character as the murderer, the planting of false clues, the use of ballistic evidence, and the extortion of a confession through a sudden psychological shock.

Poe's Dupin is only half—the amateur half—of the fictional detective, however. His professional counterpart, the police detective, arrives later, in the novels of Emile Gaboriau (1832–73). Though Dickens's Inspector Bucket and Collins's Sergeant Cuff are milestones along the road, they are not, like Gaboriau's Lecoq, the central characters of the novels in which they appear. It is Lecoq who is the first modern police detective. He calls science to his aid to examine evidence; he reasons, if less spectacularly, no less logically than Dupin; and he has at his disposal the machinery and organization of the police force.

Gaboriau, a Parisian journalist and *feuilletoniste*, first became popular with his novel *L'Affaire Lerouge*, published as a newspaper serial in 1865 (in English as *The Widow Lerouge*, 1887). Lecoq plays a very minor part here; the real detective is an amateur, old Père

Tabaret, a retired pawnbroker, whom Gaboriau occasionally makes use of later. This novel was followed by *Le Crime d'Orcival* (1867; in English as *The Mystery of Orcival*, 1887), *Le Dossier No. 113* (1867; in English as *Warrant No. 113*, 1884), and *Monsieur Lecoq* (1869; in English, 1888). Of these the best is incontestably the last. It describes Lecoq's first case, in which, aided by an unreliable, often drunk colleague suitably nicknamed Father Absinthe, he tries to establish the identity of an unknown man who has been arrested at the scene of a triple murder.

Taken together, the novels are not altogether satisfactory, partly because the portrayal of Lecoq is inconsistent—in each novel he appears as a different character—and partly because of the narrative method Gaboriau has chosen. Each novel falls into two halves: the first begins with the discovery of the crime and narrates the activities of the detective; the second, which usually takes the form of a complicated family history, describes the events leading up to the crime. But the two parts are almost independent of one another—so much so that English translations have often omitted the second part of his novels. It is all the more surprising, therefore, that Conan Doyle should have decided to adopt Gaboriau's method in three out of four of the long Sherlock Holmes stories. Only *The Hound of the Baskervilles* (1902) has a single, continuous narrative; and it undoubtedly benefits as a result.

Of course, Conan Doyle did not confine his borrowings to Gaboriau; he also borrowed Poe's detective—there is too great a similarity between the remarks and methods of Sherlock Holmes and Dupin for this to remain in doubt. The scorn which Sherlock Holmes pours on Dupin and Lecoq in the passage quoted as an epigraph to this chapter is therefore more a disingenuous attempt to keep the reader from noticing Conan Doyle's indebtedness to his predecessors than the true expression of his views. In *Memories and Adventures* (1924), he is more generous when he writes: 'Gaboriau had rather attracted me by the neat dovetailing of his plots, and Poe's masterful detective, M. Dupin, had from boyhood been one of my heroes.'

Dupin is a dilettante, an amateur detective, Lecoq a policeman, a professional. Holmes, as a 'consulting detective', represents a halfway house between the two, a professional amateur, as it were. He is paid by clients for his exertions, but is yet not part of the official police. The category is a useful one, in that it allows the establishment of three main classes of fictional detective: the professional amateur, or private detective, such as Sherlock Holmes or Hercule Poirot; the amateur amateur, or dilettante, such as Dupin or Dorothy Sayers's Lord Peter Wimsey; and the professional, or policeman, a category which can be subdivided into the professional professional, the policeman who is only a policeman, such as Lecoq or Freeman Wills Crofts's Inspector French, and the amateur professional, the policeman who is not only a policeman, such as Ngaio Marsh's Roderick Alleyn or P. D. James's Adam Dalgliesh.

It is not too difficult to distinguish between these two subdivisions, even if, in the end, the judgement is subjective. To distinguish between the professional amateur, who is employed to investigate, and the purely amateur amateur, who is not paid, but detects out of curiosity and love of the game, can be virtually impossible, however, regardless of whether objective or subjective criteria are applied. One reason for this difficulty is that authors dislike evoking an association between their private detectives and the private detective of real life, whose activities in England and America during this period consisted largely in exposing the dirty linen of divorce cases to the courts. It is understandable, therefore, that many fictional detectives should constantly reiterate their refusal to handle divorce cases, and that the financial relationship between detective and client should be slurred over or ignored. Making the detective a person of independent means, like Whitechurch's Thorpe Hazell or Ernest Bramah's Max Carrados, is a convenient way of side-stepping the issue. On the other hand, most authors must have felt an occasional twinge of doubt as to the plausibility of their amateur detectives if no reason is ever given to explain why they should constantly stumble over corpses or be repeatedly summoned to cases of mysterious death, where they are not only welcomed, but deferentially invited to the scene of the crime by the police. It follows that, although the extremes of these two classes are clear, there is a grey area in the middle populated by characters who could equally well be described as professional or amateur.

Despite its deficiencies, this classification, amplified by further subdivisions and with the addition of a final section on historical and comic detective stories and on criminals as heroes, provides the basic structure of this book. The categories are not sacrosanct, however; similar characters in different categories can be brought together, and connections across classes are made, where useful.

Since this is the history of a fictional character, rather than of a genre, it follows that the emphases will be rather different from those which might be found in a history of the detective story; also, that certain authors whose presence would certainly be expected in such a work are absent here, not because they have been considered unworthy of inclusion, but because they have not created a detective—amateur or professional—who appears with sufficient frequency to become a series character.

Chapter 2

THE PROFESSIONAL AMATEUR

When in doubt, stick to Dr Thorndyke.
(Christopher Morley)

HOLMES AND THE MAGAZINE SHORT STORY

In 1886 a newly married young doctor who had recently set up in practice in Southsea, the residential quarter of Portsmouth, submitted a short novel which had already been rejected by four or five publishers to Ward, Lock & Co. They offered him twenty-five pounds for the copyright. After some hesitation he accepted the offer, and *A Study in Scarlet* was published in *Beeton's Xmas Annual* for 1887. The doctor was, of course, Arthur Conan Doyle (1859–1930), and *A Study in Scarlet* the first appearance of Sherlock Holmes. Three other novels and five collections of short stories, the last published in 1927, make up the Sherlock Holmes canon.

In these works Conan Doyle has taken the abstract idea of the detective provided by Poe, and has fleshed out both the main figure and his surroundings. Holmes's environment is not a decaying Gothic mansion in a sketchily described Paris, a city Poe had never in fact visited, but the cosy, cluttered, late Victorian domestic interior of 221B Baker Street. His normal habitat is the streets and alleys of London, of which he has an encyclopaedic knowledge. Occasionally he ventures into the country, usually the Home Counties, though he has also penetrated as far as Devon (*The Hound of the Baskervilles*), Cornwall ('The Adventure of the Devil's Foot'), and the north of England ('The Adventure of the Priory School'). The unnamed, characterless narrator of Poe's stories has become John H. Watson, MD, late of the Army Medical Department, who, invalided home after being wounded in Afghanistan, is introduced to Sherlock Holmes in the laboratory of Bart's Hospital, and agrees to share the comfortable flat in Baker Street with him. The creation of Watson was, in fact, a stroke of genius. However outré the events he describes, the fact that they are mediated through his prosaic, stolid personality gives them a reality and a plausibility which they would otherwise lack. There are only three stories which are not narrated by Watson—one is told in the third person, the other two by Holmes himself—and all three are found in the last collection, *The Case-Book of Sherlock Holmes* (1927), universally considered the weakest, not so much for the conception of the stories as for their execution.

It is obvious from the description of Holmes in the opening chapters of *A Study in Scarlet* that Conan Doyle originally intended to make his hero much more like Dupin, to create a pure detective who would be little more than animated reason. But almost immediately human traits began to creep in. Holmes can feel emotion: annoyance, anger, chagrin. He can admire a worthy adversary, as he admires Irene Adler for outwitting him in 'A Scandal in Bohemia'. In *A Study in Scarlet* Watson describes Holmes's knowledge of literature as nonexistent; yet Holmes is soon quoting Goethe and Flaubert, quizzing Watson on his knowledge of Carlyle, and recommending to him a book he describes as 'one of the most remarkable ever penned', Winwood Reade's *Martyrdom of Man*. His corporeality and individuality are enhanced by his eccentricities. He keeps his cigars in the coal-scuttle, his tobacco in the toe end of a Persian slipper, and unanswered correspondence transfixed with a jack-knife in the centre of the mantelpiece, while the wall of his room is decorated with a patriotic V. R. done in bullet marks. Yet at the same time he is recognizably, like Dupin, a product of the Romantic tradition. He is another proud, alienated hero, superior to and isolated from the rest of humanity; a sufferer from *spleen* and *ennui*, who alleviates the deadly boredom of existence with injections of cocaine and morphine; an aesthete, a music-lover and amateur violinist who, during the intervals in the action, will drag the philistine Watson to concert hall and opera-house.

As well as introducing Holmes to the reading public, *A Study in Scarlet* made another notable contribution to the history of detective fiction: it popularized and perpetuated misuse of the term 'deduction', a misuse which is now so common as not to be worth avoiding. Strictly speaking, a deduction is an instance drawn out from a generality. If all Cretans are liars and the man before us is a Cretan, we deduce that he is a liar. This is very different from the mental leap made by Holmes when, in 'The Adventure of the Blue Carbuncle', he *infers* from the amount of dust on a hat that its owner is no longer loved by his wife. Inferences partake of the nature of all circumstantial evidence: though the degree of probability increases as each successive inference supports its predecessors, certainty can never be obtained. It is remarkable, therefore, how seldom Holmes's inferences—or deductions—prove incorrect. Indeed, they constitute his trade mark as a detective: that offhand, seemingly magical characterization of a visitor to Baker Street which then proves, on explanation, to be absurdly simple. The classical example must be the throw-away remark Holmes makes to Watson, as the latter eyes Jabez Wilson, the pawnbroker client of 'The Red-Headed League': 'Beyond the obvious facts that he has at some time done manual labour, that he takes snuff, that he is a Freemason, that he has been in China, and that he has done a considerable amount of writing lately, I can deduce nothing else.'

These showy displays of what, so Conan Doyle informs us, has come to be known as *Sherlockholmitos* [*sic*] in South America are most often irrelevant to the matter at hand; but they work marvellously well as introductions to the stories, with Holmes occasionally varying his method by exercising his deductive flair not on clients, but on objects belonging to them, such as Henry Baker's hat in 'The Adventure of the Blue Carbuncle', Grant Munro's pipe in 'The Adventure of the Yellow Face', and Dr James Mortimer's stick in *The Hound of the Baskervilles*. Once, with unhappy results, he tries his hand on Watson's watch, in *The Sign of Four* (1890).

Holmes is the first of the great detectives. He is probably the greatest of them all, and certainly the best known. He has given society its popular image of a detective: a tall, thin, eagle-eyed figure in cloak and deerstalker, with magnifying glass in one hand and pipe in the other. Yet, paradoxically, he is at the same time unique; his creation broke the mould. Any future great detective would have to be sharply differentiated from Holmes in method, appearance, eccentricity, or even nationality.

There have, of course, been many parodies, pastiches, and attempts to add to the canon—most of the last type tending to involve Holmes with either Jack the Ripper or Edward VII. Parodies range from Mark Twain's (1835–1910) 'A Double-Barrelled Detective Story' (1902), which transposes Holmes and his nephew, Fetlock Jones, to a Western setting, to Robert L. Fish's (1912–81) 1960s stories of an inept Schlock Homes and his assistant Dr Watney. The most sustained effort at pastiche is the series of stories—some seventy in all—by August Derleth (1909-71) about Solar Pons, 'the Sherlock Holmes of Praed Street', the first of which, 'The Adventure of the Black Narcissus', was written in 1928. Derleth's choice of name for his hero indicates a certain lack of empathy with the original; and, indeed, few, if any, pastiches have managed to achieve more than one of the four elements essential for a successful imitation of Doyle: authentic atmosphere, convincing plot, the Watsonian narrative tone, and an adequate amount of *Sherlockholmitos*.

Conan Doyle's great contribution to the form of the detective story genre came from his realization that, for magazine publication, a series of short stories featuring the same main character was more attractive than the traditional novel in serial form, since missing one episode of a continuous narrative deprived the reader of interest in the succeeding ones. He put the theory into practice with the first series of Sherlock Holmes stories, which began to appear in the newly founded *Strand Magazine* in 1891. The period between 1890 and the beginning of the First World War was very much a magazine age. In addition to the *Strand Magazine* there were *Pearson's*, *Cassell's*, *Harmsworth's*, the *Windsor*, and the *Royal Magazine*, all clamouring for material. And much of the fiction they published was modelled, to a greater or lesser extent, on the stories of Doyle.

HOLMES'S FIRST SUCCESSORS

The first private detective to follow Holmes was Martin Hewitt, the creation of Arthur Morrison (1863-1945), whose cases were collected in volumes such as *Martin Hewitt, Investigator* (1894) and *The Chronicles of Martin Hewitt* (1895). A civil servant who subsequently became a free-lance journalist, Morrison is best known for his stories of life in the London slums—*Tales of Mean Streets* (1894) and *A Child of the Jago* (1896). He later became an expert on Oriental art, and his book *The Painters of Japan* (1911) is still a standard reference work. Hewitt, a former solicitor's clerk who has established a private detective agency with an office near the Strand, is a stoutish man with a round, smiling face. He narrates his cases to a journalist friend, Brett, who passes them on to the reader. Sidney Paget, who illustrated Conan Doyle's stories for the *Strand Magazine* and created the definitive image of Sherlock Holmes, also illustrated the Hewitt stories; but this is the closest link between the two characters. Hewitt is a colourless figure who claims to employ 'no system beyond a judicious use of ordinary faculties', and the plots of the stories are weak.

A more interesting figure is Dorcas Dene, née Lester, heroine of *Dorcas Dene, Detective* (1897) by George R. Sims (1847–1922), a poet, playwright, novelist, short story writer, and journalist. Forced to leave the stage when her husband goes blind, Dorcas is employed as an assistant by a private detective and eventually, after his retirement, takes over the business and becomes 'a professional lady detective'. She and her husband live in a villa in Elm Tree Road, St John's Wood, together with her mother and Toddlekins, a large bulldog. Often all four join together to solve a mystery, and occasionally they are assisted by the narrator, Mr Saxon. The ideas and intrigues of the stories are no better than those of Morrison, but there is a certain freshness and liveliness about Dorcas which make her adventures reasonably readable.

A less conventional detective is Thorpe Hazell, a gentleman of independent means with an unrivalled grasp of railway details who is habitually consulted by railway companies with timetable problems or mysteries to solve. His cases, pleasantly and semi-humorously narrated by V. L. Whitechurch (1868–1933), then vicar of Blewbury near Didcot, later a canon of Christ Church, Oxford, and finally rural dean at Aylesbury, appeared in *Pearson's Magazine* and *Harmsworth's*, and in 1912 were published as a collection entitled *Thrilling Stories of the Railway*. Hazell is not interested in rolling-stock or locomotives; his forte is the study of timetables, railway lines, points, signalling procedure, and the like. He is pleasantly eccentric, a bibliophile and vegetarian dietary fanatic, whose lunch usually consists of a couple of plasmon biscuits and a glass of milk, followed by a 'chest massage' as an aid to digestion. As a detective, Hazell is a cut or two above Hewitt and Dorcas Dene. He knows about fingerprints, takes photographs of them and other evidence, is less dependent on coincidence, and uses his reasoning powers to good effect.

Carnacki, hero of *Carnacki the Ghost-Finder* (1913) by William Hope Hodgson (1877–1918), an officer in the Mercantile Marine who enlisted in the artillery at the beginning of the First World War and was killed at the battle of Ypres, is unique among fictional detectives, to my knowledge, in that he concerns himself solely with occult phenomena. He is called in to investigate hauntings, poltergeists, and other supernatural happenings, often discovering mundane explanations and criminal activity to lie behind the manifestations he witnesses. Though he uses good old-fashioned prophylactics like garlic, candles and jars of water, he does not despise modern methods, and is prepared to erect an 'electric pentacle' round the bed of a client threatened by an evil spirit. After investigating a case, he returns to his home in Cheyne Walk, Chelsea, invites his friends round, and tells them of his latest hair-raising experiences.

H. Hesketh Prichard (1876–1922) spent most of his life travelling and hunting, and utilized his experiences and knowledge of the wilderness to good effect in his stories about November Joe, a Canadian backwoodsman who is employed by the Provincial Police (*November Joe*, 1913). 'He is', the narrator is told, 'a most skilful and minute observer, and you must not forget that the speciality of a Sherlock Holmes is the everyday routine of a woodsman. Observation and deduction are part and parcel of his daily existence. He literally reads as he runs. The floor of the forest is his page.' November Joe is obviously very much in the tradition of Fenimore Cooper's heroes; the detection is solid, the plots ingenious, and the character himself pleasant and engaging. Moreover, the close contact with nature, with all the action taking place outdoors in the Canadian woods, is original and refreshing.

The pick of this small group, however, is the eponymous hero of *Max Carrados* (1914), a collection of short stories by Ernest Bramah (pseudonym of Ernest Bramah Smith, 1868–1942). Though Bramah was reticent about his private life, it appears that he was born near Manchester, tried farming for a few years, but then drifted into journalism, later becoming Jerome K. Jerome's secretary. His best-known works are the short stories relating the activities of the itinerant Chinese story-teller Kai Lung, written in a superbly polished, ludicrously exaggerated imitation of conventional Chinese modes of address and narration (*The Wallet of Kai Lung*, 1900, and other collections). His detective, Carrados, is easily distinguished from his contemporaries: he is blind. His other senses are preternaturally acute, however. Though a photograph, with its 'gelatino-chloride surface of mathematical uniformity', tells him nothing, he can get a likeness from its negative by running his fingers over the surface of the film, just as he can read letters by feeling the traces left by pen or pencil, shoot by aiming at the sound of a beating heart, and detect a false moustache from its 'five yard aura of spirit gum'. In a fascinating introduction to a later collection, *The Eyes of Max Carrados* (1923), Bramah defended himself against the accusation that he had exaggerated

Carrados's abilities, citing real-life instances of the power of the sightless to develop their other senses.

Carrados is well off, lives in 'The Turrets' in Richmond, employs a manservant named Parkinson and later a secretary named Greatorex, and often collaborates with the private detective Louis Carlyle. Bramah is by far the best writer of the five just considered, and Carrados the most plausible of the detectives. His relation with Carlyle is particularly well done, inverting, as it were, the normal relation between Holmes and Watson.

Carrados is not the only blind detective in fiction. Basil Santoine, a blind but famous American lawyer, is the central figure in *The Blind Man's Eyes* (1916) by Edwin Balmer (1883–1959) and William MacHarg (1872–1951). But Santoine's blindness is merely a disability; it is not intrinsic to the plot. More interesting, and closer in aim to Bramah, are the novels by Baynard H. Kendrick (1894–1977) about Captain Duncan Maclain, the first of which is *The Last Express* (1937). Tall, dark, and handsome, Maclain lost his sight during the First World War. He now works as a detective in New York, having learned to compensate for his blindness through his other senses, training his sense of touch, for example, by putting together complicated jigsaws, and, like Carrados, teaching himself to shoot guided by sound rather than sight.

DR THORNDYKE

Although these characters all owe much to Holmes, they are far from being his rivals. This is not true of Dr John Evelyn Thorndyke, however. Thorndyke is the most impressive and the most intellectually powerful of fictional detectives. He is lecturer—later professor—in medical jurisprudence at St Margaret's Hospital in London, and makes his first appearance in *The Red Thumb Mark* (1907). Its author, R. Austin Freeman (1862–1943), was born in Soho, the son of a tailor. After training as an apothecary, he studied medicine at the Middlesex Hospital, and qualified in 1887, the year in which he married. He was subsequently forced by lack of funds to enter the Colonial Service, and was posted to Accra on the Gold Coast. The following year he joined an expedition to the interior of Africa, of which he gives an interesting account in *Travels and Life in Ashanti and Jaman* (1898). He uses his African experience to good effect in the Rider Haggard-like adventure novel *The Golden Pool* (1905) and in the first part of *A Certain Dr Thorndyke* (1927), set in West Africa. In 1891 he was invalided home with blackwater fever, however, and thereafter he was unable to find a permanent medical position. He turned his hand to fiction, first bringing out, in collaboration with a friend, Dr J. J. Pitcairn, medical officer at Holloway Prison, *The Adventures of Romney Pringle*, published in 1902 under the pseudonym Clifford Ashdown. After the *The Red Thumb Mark* Freeman went on to produce a large number of short stories and novels with Thorndyke as detective. The first short story, 'The Blue Sequin', was published in the Christmas 1908 number of *Pearson's Magazine*. A little later he introduced an innovation into the narration of detective fiction with his invention of the 'inverted' story: in the first half the crime is shown being committed; in the second Thorndyke solves the mystery. As Freeman writes: 'The usual conditions are reversed; the reader knows everything, the detective knows nothing.' A number of inverted stories were collected in *The Singing Bone* (1912). During the First World War Freeman served in the RAMC, and thereafter produced a Thorndyke novel almost every year until his death.

There are certain similarities between Holmes and Thorndyke. Both live in central London, Holmes at 221B Baker Street, Thorndyke in chambers at 5A King's Bench Walk in the Inner Temple. Watson lives with Holmes; with Thorndyke live Polton, who is Thorndyke's laboratory assistant-cum-factotum, and Dr Christopher Jervis, a former pupil of Thorndyke, now his junior, and the narrator of a number of his cases. Like Watson in *The Sign of Four*, Jervis finds a wife in the course of the investigations of *The Red Thumb Mark*. But there is a radical difference between Holmes and Thorndyke. If Holmes's persona harks back through Dupin to the Romantic hero, Thorndyke's looks resolutely forward: he is the first truly modern, scientific detective.

When called to an investigation, he takes with him his 'portable laboratory', a small, square case covered in green Willesden canvas containing a dwarf microscope, tiny spirit-lamp, miniature reagent bottles and test-tubes, and other assorted instruments. 'The longer I practise, the more I become convinced that the microscope is the sheet-anchor of the medical jurist', he tells Jervis; and in most of his cases discovery of the criminal and proof of guilt are brought about by the careful, painstaking accumulation and combination of minute evidences. When the stories were published originally in *Pearson's Magazine*, they were accompanied by enlarged photographs of microscope slides prepared by Freeman, which purported to be those Thorndyke produced in court. They showed, for example, the difference between the root of a hair that has been torn out and one which has fallen out, or the difference between human blood and camel's blood. Unfortunately, when the stories were reprinted in book form, the illustrations were not included, presumably for reasons of expense.

That Freeman intended Thorndyke as a rival to Holmes is clear from his remarks on the genesis of the character, which contain open criticism not only of Holmes, but also of most other contemporary detectives. After pointing out that Thorndyke was not based on any real person, but deliberately invented, he continues:

As mental and bodily characters are usually in harmony, I made him tall, strong, active and keen-sighted. As he was a man of acute intellect and sound judgement, I decided to keep him free from eccentricities, such are usually associated with an unbalanced mind, and to endow him with the dignity of presence, appearance and manner appropriate to his high professional and social standing. Especially I decided to keep him perfectly sane and normal.

And in the short story 'The Anthropologist at Large' there is a not too subtle but amusing dig at Holmes's methods when a client hands Thorndyke a shabby billycock hat, saying that he understands that it is possible from the examination of a hat to deduce 'not only the bodily characteristics of the wearer, but also his mental and moral qualities, his state of health, his pecuniary position, and even his domestic relations and the peculiarities of his place of abode'—a pithy summing-up of the deductions Holmes makes from the examination of Mr Baker's hat in 'The Adventure of the Blue Carbuncle'. Thorndyke rises to the challenge, and, aided by his microscope, produces hard evidence from the hat to suggest that it belongs to a Japanese workman employed at a mother-of-pearl factory in the West India Dock Road.

There can be no doubt that Thorndyke is by far the more convincing of the two as a detective. Although Watson notes Holmes's 'profound' knowledge of chemistry, we have evidence of it only once, at the beginning of A Study in Scarlet, when Holmes announces that he has discovered a new reagent 'precipitated by haemoglobin, and by nothing else'. This is obviously fiction. By contrast, we see Thorndyke carrying out Reinsch's and Marsh's tests for the presence of arsenic, and, in order to recover the lead of a bullet from a body that has been cremated, heating the pulverized remains in a crucible together with charcoal, sodium carbonate, borax, and a couple of iron nails.

Holmes's inferences are brilliant and showy, but logically unsound; Thorndyke's arguments are rigorous, his thoughts logical and organized. In 1913 a reviewer wrote of Freeman's work:

> To read these books intelligently implies a definite exercise in the use of Mill's Canons of Inductive Logic and the books might form a very practical means of testing the student's mastery of these canons. . . . Stupid and lazy readers may be warned off, but the ordinary intelligent reader may rely upon having from Mr Freeman a course in mental gymnastics conducted under the pleasantest conditions.

Thorndyke is more knowledgeable than Holmes: he can read Egyptian hieroglyphics, identify at a glance two different types of duckweed, and explain the construction of Japanese magic mirrors. Nor does Freeman make the kind of factual mistake that occurs relatively frequently in Doyle: for example, Holmes refers to a blue carbuncle as 'crystallized charcoal', when in fact it contains no carbon; calls the snake of 'The Adventure of the Speckled Band' a 'swamp adder . . . the deadliest snake in India', although the species does not exist; describes the Japanese system of wrestling as 'baritsu', a meaningless term; and asserts that it is possible from examining the tracks left by a bicycle to tell in which direction the cyclist was going.

Thorndyke is not to everyone's taste, however. Dorothy Sayers complains that he violates the canons of 'fair-play' in the detective story. Although his finds are exhibited to the reader, their significance is not apparent unless the reader happens to share Thorndyke's specialized knowledge. The criticism seems hardly logical, since the writer must assume some knowledge on the part of the reader. It is also true that, even without Thorndyke's expertise, it is often possible to deduce the significance of the evidence from the manner in which it is exhibited. Julian Symons, who dismisses Freeman rather peremptorily in his history of crime fiction, *Bloody Murder* (1985), makes a potentially more damaging criticism when he writes that to read Freeman is 'very much like chewing dry straw'. There is some truth in this, and the early novels are also marred by some embarrassingly facetious exchanges between Thorndyke and Jervis. On the other hand, Raymond Chandler has written that Freeman is 'a much better writer than you might think, because in spite of the immense leisure of his writing he accomplishes an even suspense which is quite unexpected. . . . Freeman has so many distinctions as a technician that one is apt to forget that within his literary tradition he is a damn good writer' (*Raymond Chandler Speaking*, 1962). There is a great deal of variety in Freeman's work too, ranging from the bareness and laconicism of the short stories to the almost Gothic atmosphere of *Helen Vardon's Confession* (1922), narrated by the heroine. His villains often seem more convincingly villainous and his pictures of slum life in the East End of London more realistically squalid than their equivalent in Conan Doyle. Nevertheless, though Thorndyke might be the superior detective, Conan Doyle is undeniably the better writer. Moreover, he has unwittingly managed to give Holmes and Watson mythopoeic significance: unlike Thorndyke and Jervis, they have an existence beyond the books in which they appeared.

From about 1910 to the end of the 1920s a large number of magazine stories, especially in the United States, contained so-called scientific detectives; but their science has little or nothing in common with Thorndyke's, being largely fantastical, often, indeed, turning into pure science fiction. An exception are the early stories of Arthur B. Reeve (1880–1936) about Craig Kennedy, professor of 'criminal science' at a university in New York (*The Silent Bullet*, 1912). Here the science is usually sound, and though the author posits inventions which do not exist, such as a primitive lie-detector in the form of a chair which registers the pressure with which the arms are gripped, their construction would not have posed technological problems. Reeve deserves mention, too, for his introduction of Freud into the detection of crime; he uses 'soul analysis'—that is, psychoanalysis—in *The Dream Doctor* (1913). Later stories show a sad falling-off, though the detective became immensely popular thanks to a number of silent film serials written by Reeve, in which the heroine, Elaine, was repeatedly rescued from dreadful peril by Professor Craig Kennedy, usually nattily attired in a white laboratory coat.

Another detective of this type is Francis Lynde's (1856–1930) Calvin Sprague, a US government scientist sent west to test soils, who stops off on the way to aid a former class-mate, now general superintendent of a railway in Nevada. Six stories are included in the collection *Scientific Sprague* (1912). The railway detail is excellent.

Much later E. (1891–1973) and M. A. Radford, protesting against the fact that in crime fiction science is always the preserve of the amateur detective, wrote in the preface to their book *Inspector*

Manson's Success (1944): 'We have had the audacity—for which we make no apology—to present here the Almost Incredible: a detective story in which the *scientific* deduction by a police officer uncovers the crime and the criminal entirely without the aid, ladies and gentlemen, of any outside assistance!' The description of their policeman certainly makes it clear that he is a scientist, and it is interesting to note that he appears to have succeeded to Thorndyke's chair:

The man's face was long, with an abnormally high forehead. The eyes were set wide, and they were deep sunk. The fingers manipulating the microscope focussing wheels were long, delicate and tapering. A doctor might have said that they were the hands of a surgeon; but he would have been wrong. This was Chief Inspector Harry Manson, Doctor of Science, and Professor of Medical Jurisprudence.

But the novels themselves do not live up to this intriguing introduction.

Two other American detectives of the period preceding the First World War should be mentioned here: Fleming Stone, the scholarly, book-loving private detective who appears in novels by Carolyn Wells (1869–1942); the first is *The Clue* (1909). The detection is often sensible and the ideas ingenious, but the characters are unbelievable and the situations frequently ridiculous. Her best book is probably the non-fictional *The Technique of the Mystery Story* (1913); and her remark that 'the detective story must seem real in the same sense that fairy tales seem real to children' is often quoted.

Mary Roberts Rinehart (1876–1958) wrote some thirty crime novels, beginning with *The Circular Staircase* (1908), most of which, though well plotted, are characterized by excessive domestic detail, sentimental romantic sub-plots, and constant recourse to what Ogden Nash symbolized as the HIBK formula—'Had I but known'—which expresses the heroine's state of mind as she ruminates on her failure to act with ordinary judgement and normal caution. The author's only series detective is Nurse Hilda Adams, known as 'Miss Pinkerton', who made her first appearance in a short story entitled 'The Buckled Bag' in 1914. In the belief that a nurse can most easily penetrate a family's secrets, she is employed as an undercover operative by a Mr Potton, who, confusingly, is sometimes represented as a private detective, sometimes as a police-officer.

Of course, Freeman had introduced another innovation into the genre by giving his hero a profession which was not that of detective, but which nevertheless provided him with a more than adequate reason for indulging in detection. This has several advantages. Whether an investigation is under way or not, Thorndyke always has work; he is free of the dreadful boredom of waiting for a case to turn up, a boredom the private detective cannot escape, and one which drives Holmes to the hypodermic syringe and the seven per cent solution of cocaine. It frees him, too, from the social stigma so often attached to the profession of private detective. It is not without significance that a private detective who appears in Freeman's later novels, though honest, reliable, efficient, and devoted to Thorndyke—he saves the doctor's life at some risk to his own on one occasion—is given the unattractive, if revealing, surname of 'Snuper'.

Thorndyke is a medical jurist, both a doctor and a lawyer. He has no successors in this profession, presumably because no author since Freeman has felt competent to handle the necessary double expertise (Chief Inspector Harry Manson is of course an exception, but one doubts the genuineness of his qualifications). It is clear, however, that being a lawyer or a doctor gives a more than average chance of coming into contact with crime; hence writers since Freeman have often made their heroes practitioners of one or other of these professions. Other occupations which have proved useful in the same way are those of newspaperman, insurance investigator, and accountant. But a necessary distinction must be made between those authors who have integrated their characters' various professions into plot and narrative by usefully deploying their professional expertise and those who have, in less interesting fashion, merely used these professions as synonyms for private detective. Before turning to the private detective proper, we will consider each of these professions in turn.

LAW

Ephraim Tutt, of the New York law firm Tutt and Tutt, appears in numerous short stories by Arthur Train (1875–1945), son of the Attorney-General of Massachusetts, who studied at Harvard Law School and afterwards practised as a lawyer and assistant district attorney. The first collection of such stories is *Tutt and Mr Tutt* (1920). Tutt, who wears a stove-pipe hat, smokes stogies, plays a mean game of poker, and defends the poor and oppressed against the rich and corrupt, is described as 'a kindly old lawyer, who never yet did aught but good, although mayhap he may have done it in queer ways'. The facetiously sentimental style is a pity, for the stories can be amusing and ingenious, with good court-room scenes, while the plot often turns on some nice legal point, as when Tutt arranges for the train from Atlantic City to New York to be stopped so that a bondsman in the front half of the train is in the state of New York while the man for whom he is standing surety in the rear is still in New Jersey, with the result that the bond is forfeit.

Baroness Orczy (1865–1947), author of the Scarlet Pimpernel novels, also wrote a number of detective works, including a series of short stories about a lawyer Patrick Mulligan, known by the unlovely nickname 'Skin o' My Tooth', 'a funny looking man—just as rosy and comfortable as an Irish pig, with a face as stodgy as a boiled currant dumpling', whose moral depravity is hinted at by the fact that a French novel is always sticking out of his pocket (*Skin o' My Tooth*, 1928). The stories are pure detection, with no legal connections at all; they are told by Mulligan's confidential clerk, who gives the game away when he remarks that 'Such work as Patrick Mulligan does is more fitted to a Sherlock Holmes than to a member of so dignified a profession as the law.'

Slightly more use is made of the processes of law in the novels by H. C. Bailey (1878–1961)—better known for his Reggie Fortune stories, treated in the next section—about Joshua Clunk, the 'fashionable solicitor of the underworld', who first appears in *Garstons* (1930; US title *The Garston Murder Case*). Clunk is small and plump, with an owl-like face, sings hymns to himself in a high plaintive chirp when alone, has a passion for fruit-drops, and, as one policeman says, believes that whatever he gets up to is religious. The setting is often original, and the plots are usually complex and well worked out; but Clunk himself is too obviously an artificial collection of traits to inspire interest.

Easily the most impressive of the lawyer-detectives is Earle Stanley Gardner's (1889–1970) Perry Mason, hero of some eighty books set in and around Los Angeles, beginning with *The Case of the Velvet Claws* (1933) and ending with the posthumously published *The Case of the Postponed Murder* (1973). Like Train, Gardner was a lawyer. He was admitted to the California bar at the age of 22, and practised until 1945. The books are full of legal detail, used with great skill and ingenuity; and their climax is usually a court-room scene in which Mason, by means of brilliant cross-examination coupled with powerful and logical thought, turns the tables on his habitual adversary,

District Attorney Hamilton Burger. But Mason is more than a lawyer. Assisted by his attractive secretary, Della Street, to whom he proposes several times, always to be turned down, since she knows that marriage would be the end of their relationship, and the lanky, dyspepsia-prone private detective Paul Drake, Mason scours the city for evidence that will exonerate his clients, often sailing rather too close to the wind in the process. 'I agree that Mr Mason ought to be disbarred, but I would not have him disbarred for the world,' Dorothy Sayers commented. He faces many more difficulties than Tutt and others of the sentimental school, for his clients are by no means always wronged and innocent, and often they lie as much to him as to the police. 'My clients aren't blameless. Many of them are crooks. Probably a lot of them are guilty. That's not for me to determine. That's for the jury to determine', he tells Paul Drake. This rather more realistic view of the relationship between lawyer and client is an innovation in the genre.

Gardner also appears to be the first writer to add a romantic dimension to the detective-secretary relationship, something which was to become a cliché in the private eye novel. Finally, he brings about an important change in the relationship between unofficial and official detective. With Holmes and Thorndyke it is a relationship of co-operation between a paternalistic, superior amateur and an inferior, initially suspicious, but eventually admiring and grateful, professional. Gardner makes the relationship confrontational, however, a running feud between Mason and the official forces of law and order, represented by the district attorney, Burger, and Lieutenant Tragg of the Los Angeles police. The idea is taken up by others: treated either more seriously, as in Raymond Chandler's account of the treatment received by his detective, Philip Marlowe, at the hands of the Bay City police (in *Farewell, My Lovely*, 1940), or more humorously, as in Rex Stout's description of a similar, continuing friendly enmity between his detective, Nero Wolfe, and Inspector Cramer of the New York police. Gardner also wrote a less popular, and on the whole inferior, series of stories which treat detection from the other side of the fence. Their hero, Doug Selby, is a young Californian district attorney (*The D. A. Calls It Murder*, 1937, and others).

Arthur Crook, hero of novels by Anthony Gilbert (pseudonym of Lucy Beatrice Malleson, 1899–1973), is a burly, beer-drinking, London solicitor, coarse and somewhat shady. He wears a brown bowler hat, and first appears in *Murder by Experts* (1936). He gives little evidence of any knowledge of the law, and plausibility goes to the wall as he takes over the investigation, browbeats witnesses, and tampers with evidence, while the police look indulgently on. His American counterpart is John J. Malone, creation of Craig Rice (pseudonym of Georgiana Ann Randolph, 1908–57). Pudgy and red-faced, a cigar-smoker with a great fondness for rye whiskey, Malone is described as 'Chicago's noisiest and most noted criminal lawyer', and his manner before a jury as 'not so much technical as pyrotechnical' (*Eight Faces at Three*, 1939; UK title *Death at Three*). The reader is never privileged to see him in action, however.

Harold Q. Masur (b. 1909) uses Scott Jordan, a classical music buff and New York lawyer, as the central figure in a number of novels, beginning with *Bury Me Deep* (1947). Masur is a lawyer, and legal problems often set his plots moving. But the books really belong to the private eye category: sinuous blondes and brunettes sway in and out of the narrative; men unexpectedly come through doors with guns in their hands, and Jordan's head often collides with a blunt instrument. And, like so many private eye stories of the period, style, detail, and plot demonstrate the immense influence of Raymond Chandler.

A similar figure on the west coast of America is Simon Drake, 'part-time lawyer and full-time *bon vivant* . . . a dedicated bachelor of 35', who appears in novels by Helen Nielsen (b. 1918). These are light-hearted adventures, in which Drake displays no great amount of legal learning (*Gold Coast Nocturne*, 1951; also published as *Dead on the Level*; UK title *Murder by Proxy*). Lesley Egan (pseudonym of Elizabeth Linington, b. 1921), introduced Jesse Falkenstein, a Jewish Los Angeles lawyer with a penchant for quoting the Talmud, a gentle wife, and a mastiff, in *Against the Evidence* (1962).

Finally, three modern British writers should be noted, all of whom combine legal detail with detection. Antony Maitland, a London barrister with a game leg, who shares chambers and a house with his uncle, the famous QC Sir Nicholas Harding, is the central figure in the numerous novels by Sara Woods (1922–85)—the first is *Bloody Instructions* (1962). Michael Underwood (pseudonym of John Michael Evelyn, b. 1916), a barrister who once worked in the department of public prosecutions and author of a large number of crime novels, has more recently begun a series about a pretty young London solicitor called Rosa Epton (*The Unprofessional Spy*, 1964). And Sarah Caudwell, pseudonym of an author who read law at Oxford, was called to the Chancery bar, and practised for some years in

Lincoln's Inn, has written several books in a pleasingly mannered style—beginning with *Thus Was Adonis Murdered* (1981)—about five young members of Chancery who are assisted in investigations by their former teacher Hilary Tamar, an Oxford law professor.

MEDICINE

Reggie Fortune, MA, MB, B.Ch., FRCS, H. C. Bailey's doctor-detective, 'specialist in . . . the surgery of crime', who appears in a large number of short stories and some novels—the first collection of short stories is *Call Mr Fortune* (1920)—was immensely popular during the 1920s and 1930s, but has since been largely forgotten. Many of the stories are cleverly thought out and put together, and Reggie shows himself to be a keen observer of detail and no mean drawer of inferences—although it is his general, encyclopaedic knowledge rather than his specific medical expertise which is usually called on. 'I'm on the side of those who are wronged. I'm for the weak', he announces. The latter are most often mistreated children, when the author's genuine sympathy and indignation can occasionally overcome the detective interest in a story. Fortune's manner, his tendency in speech to elide the final *g*, his slightly patronizing attitude to the police all link him with the amiable young man-about-town group of amateur detectives. He is a more solid and weighty character, however, with a very individual, elliptical, conversational style. The following extract, addressed to Superintendent Bell and Inspector Mordan in the dining-room at Liverpool Street Station of all places, gives a good idea of both his style and his appetite:

'I don't know the cook. But let's hope for the best. A tirin' day, an active evening. Strength is what we need. Strength without somnolence. Salmon, I see. Lamb chops, I would add. One of your younger ducks would comfort me. Do you sleep after Burgundy, Inspector? A warm night, as you say. Larose is a genial claret. Let us all be genial.'

Anthony Wynne (pseudonym of Robert McNair Wilson, b. 1882), wrote a number of novels—*The Mystery of the Evil Eye* (1925) is the first—in which Dr Eustace Hailey, believed to be the fattest man in the medical profession and known as 'the Harley Street giant', is the detective and guides the steps of Inspector Biles of Scotland Yard. Hailey makes some reasonable sub-Thorndykian motions with microscope and spectroscope, and bounds about the countryside with remarkable vigour for a man of his girth. However, the medical element plays little part, and the novels, after beginning well, usually degenerate into some form of chase.

There is more detection and a more interesting, fuller use of medical detail in novels by Josephine Bell (pseudonym of Doris Bell Ball, 1897–1987) with Dr David Wintringham as the central figure. The first, *Murder in Hospital* (1937), is fresh and amusing, with pleasant romantic overtones, a supporting cast of boisterous medical students much given to practical jokes, and a particularly ingenious method of murder. Rather surprisingly, in later works the author prefers to use Wintringham purely as an amateur detective who stumbles into cases of murder without any professional involvement. In most of the novels the policeman's role is filled by Inspector Mitchell, who alternates with Wintringham as detective.

Laurence G. Blochman's (1900–75) short stories about Dr Dan Coffee, pathologist at the Pasteur Hospital in Northbank, a town in the American Mid-west—*Diagnosis: Homicide* (1950) is the first collection—also employ medical knowledge to good effect; but the one novel, *Recipe for Homicide* (1952), is a disappointment.

Psychiatrist-detectives form a sub-group within the category of doctors. Gladys Mitchell (1901–83) provided the first notable, and probably the best-known, example in the formidable person of Mrs Lestrange Bradley, consultant psychiatrist to the Home Office, author of *A Small Handbook of Psychoanalysis*, and later a Dame of the British Empire. If H. C. Bailey's reputation has declined, that of Gladys Mitchell has risen steadily since the publication of *Speedy Death* (1929), in which Mrs Bradley first startled the reader. Some sixty more books followed, in all of which Mrs Bradley acts as detective. Old on her first appearance, she never changes. She is described as 'dry without being shrivelled, and bird-like without being pretty'. She reminds some people of a pterodactyl, others of a crocodile with a sinister smile. Such a character obviously flouts convention: female detectives could be young, smart, and pretty, like Agatha Christie's Tuppence Beresford, or old, grandmotherly, and seemingly harmless, like the same author's Miss Marple. Moreover, Mrs Bradley is outrageously unorthodox in her methods: in *Speedy Death*, an extreme example perhaps, after the death of an explorer named Mountjoy, who turns out to be a woman dressed as a man, Mrs Bradley commits a second murder, is tried, acquitted, and finally admits her guilt to the defending counsel, who happens to be her son.

Though some of her deductions rest on Freudian theory, she appears to obtain her results as much by intuition—or something more. The occult—witchcraft, the supernatural, folk superstitions—perhaps plays too large a part in many of the books, to the detriment of their quality as detective stories; though this at least makes it clear that Mrs Bradley is as much a witch as a psychiatrist.

Dr Basil Willing, the psychiatrist in novels by Helen McCloy (b. 1904)—the first is *Dance of Death* (1938; UK title *Design for Dying*)—is a slightly less flamboyant character. He is a psychiatrist and criminologist who once worked in New York as a medical assistant to the district attorney's office. During the war he is in Naval Intelligence, and later he moves to Boston where he writes and lectures at Harvard. Dark and handsome, born in Baltimore to a Russian mother, he studied in Paris and Vienna, married an Austrian refugee, Gisela von Hohenems (her surname must be a tribute to Dornford Yates, who has a castle bearing the same name in his novel *Safe Custody*), and on her death is left a widower with one daughter. More orthodox than Mrs Bradley, he claims to use psychiatry not only to analyse the criminal's mind, but also to discover clues to his identity; for 'Every criminal leaves psychic fingerprints and he can't wear gloves to hide them. . . . Lies like blunders are psychological facts.'

Margaret Millar (b. 1915), who went on to produce a number of highly original, powerful crime novels, including *A Stranger in My Grave* (1960) and *How Like an Angel* (1962), started her writing career with three humorous detective stories—the first is *The Invisible Worm* (1941)—in which the police are aided by a psychiatrist whimsically called Dr Paul Prye. Apart from his name, he is memorable only for the fact that his conversation is larded with quotations from the poet William Blake.

John Creasey (1908-73), the most prolific of all crime writers, brought out under the pseudonym Michael Halliday—Kyle Hunt in the USA—a series of novels, beginning with *Cunning as a Fox* (1965), in which the central figure is Dr Emmanuel Cellini, who apparently believes he is a descendant of the great Florentine artist and sculptor Benvenuto Cellini. Described as 'more than a doctor, more than a psychiatrist, only a little less than a qualified lawyer', Cellini gives little indication of medical or psychiatric expertise, and offers his clients hardly more than sympathy and common sense.

More recently Jonathan Kellerman, professor of paediatrics at the University of Southern California, has written several powerful, exciting novels in which the detective-hero is Dr Alex Delaware, a Californian child psychologist. These effectively combine the more exotic aspects of the West Coast scene with a sympathetic portrayal of childhood stress and neurosis (*Shrunken Heads*, 1985; also as *When the Bough Breaks*).

JOURNALISM

It is surprising, in view of the unrivalled opportunity provided by journalism to delve into other people's affairs, that there are so few journalist-detectives, and that of the few there are none is particularly noteworthy.

In 1907 Gaston Leroux (1868–1927), author of *The Phantom of the Opera* (1911), brought out *La mystère de la chambre jaune* (in English as *The Mystery of the Yellow Room*, 1908), the first of several novels whose detective-hero is a young reporter on the newspaper *L'Epoque*, Joseph Rouletabille, so called because his head is as round as a billiard-ball. Rouletabille follows in the tradition of Holmes: he is much given to gnomic remarks, and has a Watson in the person of Sainclair, a Parisian lawyer, who is even more imperceptive than the original. *The Mystery of the Yellow Room* is interesting historically as an early example of the locked-room mystery, and also perhaps as the first example of a detective story in which the crime turns out to have been committed by the detective investigating it. This is not Rouletabille, but the famous police detective Frédéric Larsan, who is ultimately revealed to be also the famous criminal Ballmeyer, thus continuing the French tradition begun by Vidocq (1775–1857), who, after a career of crime, offered Napoleon his services and became the first chief of the police department.

There is a long hiatus between Rouletabille and the 1930s, when George Harmon Coxe (1901–84) began a series of novels about Kent Murdock, a press photographer who works for the *Boston Courier-Herald*, with *Murder with Pictures* (1935). This is a gangster story, strongly influenced stylistically by Dashiell Hammett. The newspaper background is credible and lively—Coxe himself worked as a reporter in the 1920s—and Murdock's photographs play an important part in the plot. Coxe also wrote numerous stories for the magazine *Black Mask* and several novels about another press photographer, Flashgun Casey, who, like Murdock, works in Boston, but for the *Express* (*Silent Are the Dead*, 1942).

Geoffrey Homes (pseudonym of Daniel Mainwaring, 1902–78), also a newspaperman, produced several novels with Robin Bishop, a reporter with a drinking problem, as their hero. Again, the atmosphere of the newsroom is well described (*The Doctor Died at Dusk*, 1936). By contrast, Dan Bannion, a reporter on the *San Francisco Journal* who appears in *The Lying Ladies* (1946) and two other novels by Robert Finnegan (pseudonym of Paul William Ryan, 1906–47), is much less of a journalist; indeed, he often seems to forget that he owes the city editor a story.

Herbert Brean (1907–73) used a free-lance magazine writer, Reynold Frame, in *Wilders Walk Away* (1948) and other novels; these are notable chiefly for the digressions on New England history, and are among the few detective stories to be furnished with footnotes. Peter Styles, the one-legged columnist for *Newsday*, hero of numerous novels by Judson Philips (b. 1903), the first of which is *The Laughter Trap* (1964), is a similar figure; but neither he nor Frame demonstrates any quality which could account for their alleged success as writers. Marginally more convincing as a pressman is Jim Qwilleran, who appears in several humorous crime novels by Lillian Jackson Braun. On his introduction, in *The Cat Who Could Read Backwards* (1966), Qwilleran is a reformed alcoholic, once a crime-reporter, who begins his rehabilitation by taking a post as art critic on a newspaper. But the real hero of the book—who reappears in the later novels—is a Siamese cat. Stretching a point, this section can be concluded with Antonia Fraser's (b. 1932) Jemima Shore, a famous television reporter, heroine of several amusing novels commencing with *Quiet as a Nun* (1977). Though sometimes incidental, the television background is used to good effect on occasion in setting the plot in motion.

INSURANCE

It is surprising, too, that authors should have neglected the possibilities offered by the world of insurance. The business not only provides countless opportunities for crime and fraud; it also gives the detective a ready-made background and excuse for existence. On the other hand, making the detective part of a large organization deprives him of his independence, his freedom to take only cases which interest him. Though few in number, insurance investigators are perhaps more notable than the journalists. Only very rarely, however, are insurance matters integrated into the plot.

Dr Thorndyke himself is the first detective with a regular insurance connection. He is permanently retained by the Griffin Life Assurance Company, and a number of his more interesting cases derive from this link. Miles Bredon, introduced in *The Three Taps* (1927), who works for the Indescribable Life Assurance Company, is the invention of Monsignor Ronald Knox (1888–1957), theologian, essayist, Bible translator, and founder of modern Sherlock Holmes studies. Bredon's insurance company, as its name suggests, is hardly to be taken seriously, and in all the books insurance questions merely provide a pretext for the beginning of an investigation. However, the detection is usually reasonable, and the by-play between Bredon and his wife Angela, who accompanies him on most of his investigations, amusing and witty. The same adjectives apply to *Fast Company* (1938), set in New York, by Marco Page (pseudonym of Harry Kurnits, 1909–68), in which Joe Glass doubles as a rare-book dealer and an investigator for an insurance company. There is much expertise on the antiquarian book trade, a good deal of action, and a dialogue which crackles and sparkles like the best Hollywood comedy. Doris Disney's (1907–76) first novel about Jeff DiMarco, claims-adjuster for a New England insurance company, *Dark Road* (1946; also published as *Dead Stop*), is of the inverted type, with a negligible insurance element. Insurance is far more important, however, in Macdonald Hastings's (1909–82) novels about Montague Cork, general manager of the Anchor Accident Insurance Company (*Cork on the Water*, 1951; also in US as *Fish and Kill*), in which an insurance claim is often the fulcrum of the intrigue. But these stories are more adventure than detection. Their interest lies in their settings, the varied and eccentric cast of characters, and Mr Cork himself, a prim but engaging martinet, who, according to the author, was based on Claude Wilson, a former managing director of the Cornhill Insurance Company in London.

Harry Carmichael (pseudonym of Leopold Horace Ognall, 1908–79) wrote a long series of books, beginning with *Death Leaves a Diary* (1952), about John Piper, an insurance assessor, who often works with Quinn, a drunken, seedy crime-reporter on a London paper. But, although insurance matters often provide the initial impetus to the narrative, they usually fade into the background as the book progresses, and it becomes a normal detective story. Some of the novels are more violent than the usual run, and seem to represent an attempt to transpose the American private eye novel to an English setting.

M. E. Chaber (pseudonym of Kendell Crossen, 1910–81) has written novels about Milo March, once with the OSS, now an insurance investigator in Denver, Colorado—*Hangman's Harvest* (1952) is the first—but these are thrillers rather than detective stories. Finally, Joseph Hansen (b. 1923) has used Dave Brandstetter, an insurance investigator for the Californian company Medallion Life, as the hero of a number of novels, beginning with *Fadeout* (1970). Again, insurance is only a means of getting the story going; what makes the novels unusual is that Brandstetter is homosexual, a bold stroke on the part of the author, given the aggressive heterosexuality of much American detective fiction.

ACCOUNTANCY

Again a trick seems to have been missed here. The accountant can come across as much fraudulent activity as the insurance investigator, though he is perhaps less likely to encounter murder. At the same time he can be much more of a free agent. Yet only two authors worth noting have made use of the profession. Both are accountants themselves, and both employ intricacies of income tax or company balance sheets to good effect. David Dodge (b. 1910) uses a Californian accountant, Whit Whitney, in a series of books—*Death and Taxes* (1941) is the first. Clark Smith (b. 1919), author of a textbook on internal auditing, puts Nicky Mahoun, a chartered accountant, into several novels; in *The Speaking Eye* (1955) Mahoun investigates fraud in a company near Glasgow. Like Carmichael, Smith, who has obviously been influenced by Raymond Chandler, tries to create a hero akin to the tough American private eye, with, at times, an unintentionally comic result.

THE SCHISM OF THE 1920s

Early in the 1920s a new type of fictional detective came into being in the United States. Whereas the conventional private detective always has literary antecedents, going back to Sherlock Holmes and, through him, to Dupin, even if the connection is attenuated at times, the new type, variously called private investigator, private eye, or, colloquially, hard-boiled dick, is the product of American reality. Sometimes he belongs to a detective agency, thereby owing his origin to the Pinkerton Agency, founded by Scotsman Allan Pinkerton (1819–84) in 1850—its emblem was an open eye, with the motto 'We Never Sleep', whence the pun on private eye. Sometimes he is a lone individual, a modern knight, defending the helpless and oppressed. But in both cases the gangsters, the violence, and the gun-play reflect American life during and after Prohibition.

Though similar superficially, the private detective and the private eye are radically opposed to one another. Perhaps the best way to illustrate the main differences between them is schematically, in tabular form.

Private detective	*Private eye*
Rural or urban setting	Urban setting
Closed society, with limited number of suspects, who are introduced at the beginning of the narrative	Open society, with indefinite number of suspects, who are introduced throughout the narrative
Detective is usually hired to solve a crime	Detective is usually hired to investigate a situation
Detective often has an assistant with whom he has a Holmes–Watson relationship	Detective may have colleagues or a devoted secretary
Detective basically static: remains in one place to interview suspects	Detective basically mobile; moves from place to place to interview characters
Detective and police co-operate	Detective and police usually antagonists
Police usually honest	Police often corrupt
Little violent action, and confined to the conclusion if it occurs	Much violent action throughout narrative
Organized crime rare	Organized crime common
No sex; love interest only between minor characters	Sex; love interest between detective and client or detective and secretary
Intake of alcohol normal	Intake of alcohol excessive
Third-person narration or first-person narration by Watson-type figure	Usually first-person narration by detective

Attempts have occasionally been made to transplant the private eye to British soil—two such have been mentioned above. But the graft has never taken: the private eye remains essentially American. The private detective, on the other hand, has flourished equally on both sides of the Atlantic.

THE PRIVATE DETECTIVE: 1920 TO THE PRESENT

In 1920 an author who has been outsold only by Shakespeare and the Bible and whose detective was, after Sherlock Holmes, to become the best known in the world, brought out her first book, *The Mysterious Affair at Styles*. In creating Hercule Poirot, Agatha Christie (1890–1976) gave him far too many extravagant characteristics, and made almost every mistake possible in setting up a series character. Poirot is old, having retired from the Belgian police some years before. His appearance is odd: he is only five feet four in height; his head is shaped exactly like an egg; and he has a stiff, military moustache. He also has a limp when he makes his first appearance, although this is later forgotten. He has a number of eccentricities: he is obsessively neat and tidy, loves symmetry, constantly rearranges ornaments, and builds card houses at moments of tension. Worst of all, he is Belgian, which means that he must speak in a vaguely broken English interlarded with French phrases. Like Holmes, he is provided with an assistant-cum-narrator, Captain Hastings, who, like Watson, has been invalided out of the Army. Hastings, impenetrably stupid and ineffably self-satisfied, does not appear in all Christie's Poirot stories, however. The author's own feelings about Poirot emerge clearly through the humorous self-caricature she offers in later books with the figure of the detective-novelist Ariadne Oliver, an untidy, middle-aged lady who has unwisely saddled herself with an appalling incubus in the form of a disastrously misconceived Finnish detective.

Though Poirot may be almost as well known as Holmes, he has never attracted attention and affection in the way his predecessor has. No scholarship has been devoted to the incidents of his life; and it has even gone largely unnoticed that Agatha Christie has carelessly domiciled him sometimes in Whitehaven, sometimes in Whitehouse, and sometimes in Whitefriars Mansions. Whereas Conan Doyle's stories would collapse without Holmes, Poirot is less essential to the novels in which he appears, for it is the puzzle, together with the sleight of hand by which Agatha Christie diverts suspicion from one character to another, which are important. Indeed, when the author adapted her novels for the stage, she often removed Poirot from the plot altogether.

A *Mysterious Affair at Styles* was a landmark, however. Poirot was an original character; the writing has life and sparkle; the narration is short and succinct; and the method of murder—bromide is added to a tonic containing strychnine, thereby precipitating the strychnine and making the last dose fatal—is ingenious. Like one of her characters, Agatha Christie had worked in a hospital dispensary during the war, and her use of poison is always technically sound. These qualities are rare among Agatha Christie's successors in the 1920s and 1930s. Their works tend to be long-winded and overburdened with irrelevant romance or implausible melodrama.

Agatha Christie produced a more convincing amateur detective, and one, moreover, who was far more successfully integrated into setting and plot, in Miss Jane Marple, the elderly spinster who makes her first appearance in *The Murder at the Vicarage* (1930). Apparently based to some extent on the author's own grandmother, Miss Marple lacks the extravagances of Poirot, who, by contrast, seems a figure who has been conceived abstractly, as a theoretical exercise. She observes keenly and deduces soundly, drawing for her knowledge of human duplicity and evil on a lifetime spent watching the inhabitants of St Mary Mead, the small village in which she lives.

A very similar character is Patricia Wentworth's (pseudonym of Dora Amy Turnbull, 1878–1961) Miss Maud Silver, who has a lengthy career as a professional detective, beginning with *Grey Mask* (1928), the title of which refers to an arch-criminal who uses an indiarubber mask to conceal his features from his subordinates. Miss Silver, who knits a great deal, holding her needles in the German fashion, while listening to her clients' confidences, is less individual and less perspicacious than Miss Marple; and most of the stories in which she appears are half detection, half romance. Both ladies may possibly owe something to Miss Climpson, the middle-aged spinster occasionally employed as an assistant by Lord Peter Wimsey, Dorothy Sayers's detective. The unique advantages which such characters bring to detection are expounded by Wimsey, who speaks of 'thousands of old maids, simply bursting with useful energy . . . [whose] magnificent gossip powers and units of inquisitiveness are allowed to dissipate themselves'.

A more conventional detective is Colonel Gore, hero of *The Deductions of Colonel Gore* (1924; also published as *The Barrington Mystery*), by Lynn Brock (pseudonym of Alister McAllister, 1877–1943). Although an amateur in this first book, by the second he has established a detective agency. Gore, lean, bronzed, and ex-Indian Army, is not too far removed from cliché, and as a detective proceeds mainly by guesswork. The plots are hideously complex, however: *Colonel Gore's Second Case* (1926) has a twenty-five-page appendix in fine print to clear up unexplained details. Another ex-Army gentleman is Philip MacDonald's (1899–1981) Colonel Gethryn, an old Secret Service hand who retains some undefined connection with the police and is continually called upon to pull their chestnuts out of the fire. Gethryn, whose career extends from *The Rasp* (1924) to *The List of Adrian Messenger* (1959), has always been the more popular and better known of the two, but his grasp of consecutive reasoning is as hazy as Gore's, and the latter's company is perhaps to be preferred.

At about this time Edgar Wallace (1875–1932) dashed off a number of stories about Mr J. G. Reeder, a private detective attached to the public prosecutor's office, the best of which are collected in *The Mind of Mr J. G. Reeder* (1925). Reeder was conceived rather along Poirot lines, it seems, on the assumption that the person who looks least like a detective makes the most striking one. In his fifties, he is small with mutton-chop whiskers, wears steel-rimmed pince-nez, a frock coat, and a high, flat-crowned bowler hat. He is a timid man, who always carries a tightly furled umbrella with a knife blade in the handle and has a revolver in an inner pocket. He has an extraordinary memory for faces, and attributes his success as a detective to the fact that he has 'the mind of a criminal'.

Far less interesting—indeed, almost completely unmemorable apart from the fact that he reads William James—is the London private detective Philip Tolefree, who specializes in financial crime: he appears in *The Fatal Five Minutes* (1932) and other novels by R. A. J. Walling (1869–1949). Nor can much be said for Ronald Camberwell of the Chaney and Camberwell Detective Agency, hero of a number of novels by J. S. Fletcher (1863–1935), most of which degenerate into melodrama—*Murder at Wrides Park* (1931) is the first. In fact, Fletcher's earlier novels—he wrote over a hundred in all—are preferable. His main claim to fame, however, is that he was Woodrow Wilson's favourite detective story writer. An oddity is Sir George Bull, the detective in two novels by Milward Kennedy (pseudonym of

Milward Rodon Kennedy Burge, 1894–1968): *Bull's Eye* (1933) and *Corpse in Cold Storage* (1934). Bull is a confidence man who assumes the role of a private detective in order to gain entrance to a wealthy household. Once there, he finds himself unwillingly obliged to act the part in earnest. The books are amusing, with reasonable detection; and Bull is notable for being one of the few private detectives to drink as much as an abstemious private eye.

The outstanding British private detective of the 1930s, however, is Nigel Strangeways, who takes his name from the famous Manchester prison. The creation of Nicholas Blake (pseudonym of Cecil Day Lewis, 1904–72, Poet Laureate from 1968), he makes his entrance in *A Question of Proof* (1935), the story of a murder at a boys' preparatory school. After being sent down from Oxford for answering examination papers in limericks, Strangeways travelled for some time, and then began work as a private detective, with immense success. His career is facilitated by the fact that he is the nephew of the assistant commissioner of Scotland Yard. He is tall and thin, looks like an unsuccessful bust of T. E. Lawrence, and has few eccentricities apart from an inordinate thirst for tea and an inability to sleep unless heavily covered with blankets. He marries an explorer, Georgia Cavendish, and after her death in the Second World War forms a liaison with a sculptor, Clare Massinger. At his best, Strangeways is hard to surpass. The reasoning is close and acute, the deductions genuine. Although he bears some resemblance to the young man-about-town group of amateur detectives to be discussed in the following chapter, his facetiousness conceals a more serious nature. Further, the suspects and murderers are far better developed as characters, with a deeper, more complex psychology. But the quality of the stories is uneven, the least satisfactory, perhaps, being the novels which most approximate thrillers, such as *The Sad Variety* (1964).

During this period, presumably because of the dominance of the private eye, far fewer private detectives emerged in the United States. In the 1920s only Octavus Roy Cohen's (1891–1959) Jim Hanvey is worth noting. He is an obese New York private detective with glabrous grey eyes, who patiently wears his victims down. A number of the best short stories about him are collected in *Jim Hanvey, Detective* (1923).

The next decade was marked by the appearance of America's best-known private detective, when Rex Stout (1886–1975) brought out *Fer-de-Lance* (1934), and introduced Nero Wolfe to the public for the first time. By birth a Montenegrin, Wolfe weighs a seventh of a ton, and lives in a brownstone on West 35th Street in New York. His twin passions are food, provided by his Swiss chef, Fritz Brenner, and orchids, which he grows in a conservatory on his roof. He dislikes exerting himself, and accepts cases only when financially pressed. His assistant, who is also the narrator of all his cases, is Archie Goodwin, whose main interests apart from detection are young women and dancing. Of all detectives Wolfe is the closest to Holmes: not Sherlock, however, but his brother Mycroft. The latter is described by Doyle as 'absolutely corpulent' and having a 'massive' head, while Sherlock remarks of him in 'The Adventure of the Greek Interpreter' that 'If the art of detection began and ended in reasoning from an armchair, my brother would be the greatest criminal agent that ever lived.' But this is a perfect description of Wolfe. While Archie pounds the streets, doing the necessary legwork, Wolfe, who only ever leaves his house under duress, sits in his specially built office chair, pushing his lips in and out, until he arrives at a solution through pure ratiocination. The detection is never less than satisfactory, and can reach great heights, though the form of the novels is slightly repetitive: they usually end with a gathering of the suspects in Wolfe's office, at which Wolfe exposes the criminal and turns him over to Inspector Cramer of the New York Police Department. Further, at times it is difficult not to feel that the author has been unduly constrained by the need to respect Wolfe's eccentricities. All in all, though, he is a magnificent creation, and the household at West 35th Street, like that at 221B Baker Street, has a solidity and reality which transcend the boundaries of fiction.

The next thirty years are dominated by the private eye. Of the new private detectives to appear during this period, only a few are worth noting. Fergus O'Breen is an exuberant, red-headed Irish detective who works in Los Angeles and appears in novels by Anthony Boucher (pseudonym of William Anthony Parker White, 1911–68), a critic and editor of crime fiction (*The Case of the Crumpled Knave*, 1939). H. C. Branson's (b. 1924) John Bent is a quiet, bearded medical man turned detective who drinks a great deal of bourbon and solves crimes through a kind of osmotic process (*I'll Eat You Last*, 1941, also published as *I'll Kill You Last*). Hilda Lawrence's (b. 1906?) Mark East is a Manhattan private detective who is usually aided by two peculiar spinsters from upstate New York, Bessy Petty and Beulah Pond (*Blood upon the Snow*, 1944). Beverley Nichols's (1898–1983) Horatio

Green, who is small and plump, has a 'refined olfactory sense' which enables him to recognize a person's race by his body odour. He also has perfect musical pitch, a 'curious power of healing' in his fingers, and is a water diviner (*No Man's Secret*, 1954).

At the beginning of the 1970s, however, P. D. James (b. 1920) gave the genre a new direction with *An Unsuitable Job for a Woman* (1972), in which she introduced Cordelia Gray, a self-reliant, independent-minded 22-year-old who inherits the tiny Soho detective agency in which she has been working after its owner commits suicide. A character very much in the same mould is Anna Lee, an ex-policewoman who works for a London detective firm and appears in *Dupe* (1980) and other novels by Liza Cody. Two other recent, original detectives are Manuel Vazquez Montalban's (b. 1939) Pepe Carvalho, who works in Barcelona and is as much of a gastronome as Nero Wolfe (*Los Mares del Sur*, 1979; in English as *Southern Seas*, 1986), and Dan Kavanagh's (pseudonym of Julian Barnes, b. 1946) Duffy, a bisexual ex-policeman with a stud in one ear who runs a one-man security firm in London (*Duffy*, 1980).

THE PRIVATE EYE FROM WILLIAMS TO WARSHAWSKI

If the era of Prohibition, with its lawlessness, gangsters, and corrupt police, provided the reality from which the private eye sprang, it was the pulp magazines which made him popular. Seven by ten inches, with a lurid glossy cover and some 120 pages of cheap, wood-pulp paper, the pulp magazine had first appeared towards the end of the previous century. During the 1920s and 1930s, however, titles proliferated and circulations soared. A number were devoted entirely to crime fiction, including *Detective Story*, founded during the First World War; *Detective Fiction Weekly* and *Clues* of the 1920s; and *Dime Detective*, *Thrilling Detective*, *Spicy Detective*, and *Crimebusters* of the 1930s. The most famous and the best was *Black Mask*, founded in 1920 by H. L. Mencken and George Jean Nathan to take stories which their other magazines, such as *Smart Set*, could not use. Taken over in the same year by the Warner Publishing Company, it became a crime magazine. Its best years were from 1926 to 1936, when it was edited by Captain Joseph T. Shaw (1874–1952).

The first hard-boiled detective, private eye story is generally supposed to be 'The False Burton Combs' by Carroll John Daly (1889–1958), published in *Black Mask* in 1922. The unnamed narrator is not strictly a detective, but a gun-for-hire living on the borders of the world of crime. In the following year, however, 'Knights of the Open Palm' (*Black Mask*, 1923) introduced Daly's best-known detective, Race Williams, who appears in seven novels—*The Snarl of the Beast* (1927) is the first—and numerous short stories. To create him, Daly simply moved the cowboy hero off the prairie and on to the streets of New York or Chicago. Tough, fearless, and violent, Williams carries two revolvers, is fast on the draw, and a wonderful shot: once he fires both guns simultaneously yet makes only one hole between the eyes of the victim. He has little respect for the law; he has his own code, and deals out his own brand of frontier justice, usually a bullet in the brain. A constant opponent is Florence Drummond, also known as The Flame or The Girl with the Criminal Mind. There is a good deal of sadism about the violence, which goes together with an unpleasant streak of sentimentality. Although later writers moved away from Daly's model, its values were revived by Mickey Spillane (b. 1918), who significantly gives his first book about Mike Hammer, toughest of all private eyes, the title *I, the Jury* (1974), and ends the novel with Hammer executing a naked woman, the beautiful blonde psychiatrist who has been pursuing him throughout the book and is the murderer of his crippled friend.

In October 1923 *Black Mask* published 'Arson Plus', a short story about an unnamed short, tubby, 40-year-old detective who works for the Continental Detective Agency in San Francisco. The story was signed Peter Collinson, a pseudonym used by Dashiell Hammett (1894–1961). More stories about the Continental Op followed (most are collected in *The Big Knockover*, 1966), including two novels, *Red Harvest* (1929) and *The Dain Curse* (1929), which Hammett later called 'a silly story'. Hammett himself had worked for the Pinkerton Detective Agency, first in Baltimore, later in San Francisco. His detective is modelled on his superior in Baltimore, Jimmy Wright, while the manager of the Continental Op's agency, an old man who has been in the business all his life and of whom his operatives boast that he can 'spit icicles in July', is based on Hammett's boss in San Francisco, Phil Geauque. The Op is the first professional private eye. He enjoys being a detective. For eighteen years, he says, 'I've been getting my fun out of chasing crooks and solving riddles . . . I can't imagine a pleasanter future than twenty-some years more of it.' Hammett also drew on his own experience for the characters and events of the stories; and his crooks are a particularly colourful and evocatively named crowd. He comes much closer to reality than most of his contemporaries, and avoids the melodrama of Daly's stories. Yet at the same time the amount of action and violence verges on the implausible: fists fly, machine-guns stutter, and bodies pile up. In 'The Big Knockover' the body count gets into the hundreds as an army of gangsters sack the business centre of San Francisco and then kill each other off in their greed for the loot. Exaggerations of this kind, even more obvious in *The Dain Curse*, make it hard to believe that Hammett is not poking a little sly fun at the genre. This seems especially true of 'Corkscrew', a rather poor story which reverses Daly's method by putting the urban detective back into the Western. Corkscrew is a small Arizona cow town which the Op, acting as deputy sheriff, cleans up in the traditional manner. There is a certain comedy too—though Hammett does not make too much of it—in the way his detective, while continually complaining that he is too old and out of shape for this work, takes enough punishment to put the fittest of young men into intensive care. What is most notable about the stories, however, is their style. They are narrated by the detective in a stripped-down, stark language which is objective and unemotional, like that of a report on the case written for the agency.

Better known than the Continental Op is Sam Spade, the detective in only one of Hammett's novels, *The Maltese Falcon* (1930), made famous by John Huston's film of 1941 with Humphrey Bogart as Spade. Hammett later wrote of Spade that he was 'idealized . . . in the sense that he is what most of the private detectives I've worked with would like to have been'. The typical detective, he went on, wants to be a 'hard and shifty fellow, able to take care of himself in any situation, able to get the best of anybody he comes in contact with'. Brilliant as it is, *The Maltese Falcon* sits uneasily within the private eye genre. In a sense it is a dead end; Spade has no successors. This seems partly due to the fact that Hammett has taken the cool clinical style of the Continental Op stories one logical step further by narrating the novel in the third person. He describes in detail Spade's everyday actions—how he dresses, pours a drink, rolls and lights a cigarette—but never reveals his thoughts or emotions, apart from what can be gleaned from his words or the expression on his face. The reader cannot empathize with him or vicariously experience his fear or excitement or pain. And at times the careful, pedantic precision of Hammett's style seems to lapse into self-parody, as in his description of Spade making a midnight snack: 'He spread liverwurst on, or put cold corned beef between, the small ovals of bread he had sliced.'

Jonathan Latimer (1906–83) produced a series of original novels with the New York private eye Bill Crane as their hero. The first, *Murder in the Madhouse* (1935), begins with Crane being committed to a lunatic asylum. It is only towards the end of the book that the reader is told that Crane is a private detective who is carrying out an investigation. There's a pleasingly cynical, slightly bawdy tone to Latimer's books, and the prevailing mood is one of slightly drunken irresponsibility. Crane spends most of his time in an alcoholic haze, which does not seem to affect his deductive abilities, however.

In an attack on the artificiality of the traditional detective story, Raymond Chandler (1888–1959) wrote that Dashiell Hammett 'gave murder back to the kind of people that commit it for reasons, not just to provide a corpse, and with the means at hand, not with hand-wrought duelling pistols, curare, and tropical fish'. At the same time he felt that more could be done with the language in which Hammett had written; it could be made to 'say things he did not know how to say or feel the need of saying. In his hands it had no overtones, left no echo, evoked no image beyond a distant hill.' Born in Illinois, Chandler was brought up in England. He fought in the First World War, and then returned to America, settling in California, where he became a successful executive in an oil company. In 1932 he was sacked for drunkenness, and turned to writing for pulp magazines, publishing his first story in 1933. In the early stories and novelettes—which he was later to cannibalize for his novels—he gradually developed the figure of his detective, who emerged as Philip Marlowe in *The Big Sleep* (1939). Marlowe lives in Los Angeles, is 33 on his first appearance, tall, and handsome. He once worked as an investigator for the district attorney, but was sacked for insubordination. He does chess problems for relaxation, and, more cultured than most of his colleagues, listens to classical music and can quote from Browning, Eliot, and Flaubert. It is undeniable that with the seven Marlowe novels—even though *Playback* (1958) is a failure and *The Long Goodbye* (1953) weak—Chandler had, as he wrote, 'taken a cheap, shoddy and utterly lost kind of writing and . . . made of it something that intellectuals claw each other about'. Yet in the process he had romanticized—and to a certain extent sentimentalized—the image of the private eye which he had taken over from Hammett. Spade is not a pleasant character: he will pursue his own advantage or defend himself with equal ruthless selfishness. Marlowe, by contrast, is pleasant, sympathetic, and most of all, selfless. With a high sense of obligation to his clients, he is willing to sacrifice himself for their sake. He, like Spade, is idealized, but as a perfect man, not a perfect private detective; he is an amalgam of knight and father confessor, with touches of sainthood. Chandler made his intentions perfectly clear in a famous passage of his essay 'The Simple Art of Murder' (1944), in which he writes:

Down these mean streets a man must go who is not himself mean, who is neither tarnished nor afraid. . . . He must be a complete man and a common man and yet an unusual man. He must be . . . a man of honour, by instinct, by inevitability, without thought of it, and certainly without saying it. He must be the best man in his world and a good enough man for any world.

It is this image, rather than Hammett's more realistic one, which was to dominate in later private eye fiction.

Earle Stanley Gardner, writing as A. A. Fair, produced a number of novels—the first is *The Bigger They Come* (1939; UK title *Lam to the Slaughter*)—about an unusual couple of private investigators, Bertha Cool and Donald Lam. They are out of the ordinary in that they are partners, in contrast to most private eyes who are isolated, lonely, Romantic heroes, and in that the normal male-female relationship is inverted, Bertha Cool being large, tough, and the one who runs the business, and Lam, a disbarred lawyer who narrates the novels, her small, gentle assistant. The plots, like those of the Perry Mason stories, are full of ingenuity, and the tone is light and amusing.

With Hammett and Chandler the private eye story had reached its apogee. During the next decade there followed a procession of epigones, usually distinguishable from one another only by the city in which they work. Moreover, as the detective lost his individuality, the plot lost its interest and originality, becoming merely the means for linking together a series of ritual encounters. Henry Kane (b. 1918) has Peter Chambers, his New York 'private richard', give a mildly funny send-up of the formula in *Armchair in Hell* (1948):

He drinks, drinks more, and more; flirts with women, blondes mostly, who talk hard but act soft, then he drinks more, then, somewhere in the middle, he gets dreadfully beaten about, then he drinks more, then he says a few dirty words, then he stumbles around, punch-drunk-like, but he is very smart and he adds up a lot of two's and two's, and then the case gets solved.

At this point, therefore, the history of the genre perforce degenerates into not much more than a bare list of names. Desmond Shannon, a huge Irishman with red hair, works for an agency in New York with a prim, middle-aged secretary (*Fugitive from Murder*, 1940). The author is M. V. Heberden (b. 1906), whose initials, perhaps surprisingly, stand for Mary Violet. Brett Halliday's (pseudonym of Davis Dresser, 1904–77) Michael Shayne, as tall and red-haired as Shannon, but rangy and angular, lives in Miami (*Dividend on Death*, 1939); Cleve F. Adams's (1895–1949) Rex McBride, another Irishman, but black-haired, in California (*Sabotage*, 1940; also as *Death Before Breakfast*; UK title *Death at the Dam*). Bill Lennox, a trouble-shooter for General Consolidated Studios who appears in novels by Willis Todhunter Ballard (1903–80), works in Hollywood and later in Las Vegas (*Say Yes To Murder*, 1942; also as *The Demise of a Louse*, under the pseudonym John Shepherd). Frank Kane's (1912–68) Johnny Liddell begins as an operative for the Acme Detective Agency in New York, but then acquires an office of his own in Manhattan, as well as an attractive, red-haired secretary called Pinky (*About Face*, 1947; also as *Death About Face* and as *The Fatal Foursome*). Wade Miller's (pseudonym of Robert Wade, b. 1920, and Bill Miller, 1920–61) Max Thursday works in San Diego (*Guilty Bystander*, 1947), Bill S. Ballinger's (1912–80) Barr Breed in Chicago (*The Body in the Bed*, 1948).

In 1949 Ross Macdonald (pseudonym of Kenneth Millar, 1915–83) brought out *The Moving Target* (originally published under the pseudonym of John Macdonald; reissued later, after the film with Paul Newman, with the title *Harper*), the first of what was to become a series of some nineteen novels in which the detective-hero is Lew Archer. With its appearance, it seemed that Hammett and Chandler had at last found a successor. Like Hammett's and Chandler's heroes, Archer lives and works in California. He is much closer to Marlowe than to the Continental Op or Spade, however. He is in his mid-thirties and more cultured than Marlowe, with literary and artistic interests. He was once a policeman in Long Beach, but was fired for refusing to work for a corrupt force. He is separated from his wife, who, like the wives of so many private eyes and policemen, cannot accept the way in which his work intrudes on their private life.

Chandler himself was carpingly critical of the novel, finding the language pretentious and the story empty. His comments are perhaps unfair; but to read Macdonald is to see that a great deal has happened to the language of the private eye novel since the stark, pared-down formulations of the Continental Op stories. In Hammett's hands the style was classical; Chandler made it romantic; but with Macdonald it has become decadent. His pages consist of a constant succession of striking images, which, in the later books, often seem over-explicit or over-emphasized. At the same time, as the novels progress, it becomes more and more obvious that Macdonald is using the private eye formula as a vehicle for his obsession with the breakdown of the family in Californian society: crime becomes a symptom, rather than the illness. It is no wonder that we find Archer using the jargon of psychology—'I felt I was beginning to get the Gestalt of the case', he says—for he is becoming more a psychotherapist than an investigator. And the image of the detective changes in consequence. If Hammett idealized the detective as the perfect private eye and Chandler as the perfect man, Macdonald idealizes him as the perfect parent, a surrogate father for the abandoned children he meets. The idea of detection as paid work has almost completely vanished. 'I took the money, since I needed it for expenses, but I felt vaguely declassed by the transaction, like a repossession man', Archer remarks. We have come a long way since Sam Spade screwed Brigid O'Shaughnessy's last dollar out of her, and then told her to hock her jewels if she needed money.

While Macdonald led the tradition away on an ultimately abortive mission towards social psychology, it continued elsewhere in more orthodox fashion. Bart Spicer's (b. 1918) Carney Wilde works in Philadelphia (*The Dark Light*, 1949), Richard S. Prather's (b. 1921) Shell Scott, a former marine with white, short-cropped hair, in Hollywood (*Case of the Vanishing Beauty*, 1950). Manny Moon, the Californian detective in books by Richard Deming (1915–83), is differentiated from his fellows by his artificial foot (*The Gallows in my Garden*, 1952). Michael Avallone (b. 1924), using no less than twelve different pseudonyms, has produced over thirty novels about New York detective Ed Noon, a movie and baseball buff (*The Spitting Image*, 1953). Thomas B. Dewey (b. 1915) writes of a Chicago private eye known only as Mac, and pays explicit tribute to Chandler when he gives one of his novels the title *The Mean Streets* (1955). A similar tribute is paid by Milton Lesser (b. 1928), who adopts the pseudonym Stephen Marlowe for his stories about Chester Drum, a private eye in Washington D. C. whose cases often involve espionage (*The Second Longest Night*, 1955). Another admirer of Chandler is William Campbell Gault (b. 1910), who inserts oblique references to the master's work in his excellent novels about football-player turned detective Brock 'the Rock' Callahan, a former guard with the Los

Angeles Rams (*Ring Round Rosa*, 1955; also as *Murder in the Raw*).
The idea that brawn does not necessarily negate brain has been taken
up more recently by Joe Gores (b. 1931), who uses an ex-Notre Dame
football-player, nose-guard Bonecrack Krajewski, as the detective in
the short story 'Smart Guys Don't Snore' (1987). Basil Copper
(b. 1924), a British author, has portrayed the Los Angeles scene convincingly in his Mike Faraday stories (*The Dark Mirror*, 1966).
Michael Collins (pseudonym of Dennis Lynds, b. 1924) uses a one-
armed hero, Dan Fortune, born Fortunowski, who operates a
detective agency in the Chelsea district of New York (*Act of Fear*,
1967). William F. Nolan (b. 1928) is best known for blending crime
and science fiction, as in *Logan's Run* (1967) and the comic *Space for
Hire* (1971), in which private eye Sam Space from Mars is hired by a
beautiful three-headed Venusian; but he has also written novels set
in Southern California about a more normal detective, Bart Challis
(*Death is for Losers*, 1968).

By the 1970s, as Macdonald's books became more and more case
histories, and less and less histories of cases, the genre began to lose its
reproductive capability. Some writers retreated into the past; thus
Andrew Bergman's detective in *The Big Kiss-Off of 1944* (1974), the
balding, Jewish Jack LeVine, gets involved in Dewey's campaign
against Roosevelt. Others turned to pastiche. Thus Spenser, the
Boston private eye who is the hero of Robert B. Parker's (b. 1932) *The
Godwulf Manuscript* (1973), has, like Marlowe, a name taken from
English literature and a girl-friend called Loring; and, like Marlowe,
was fired for insubordination. But his card has crossed daggers where
Marlowe's had a tommy-gun.

In an attempt to restore the genre's vitality, detectives were given
more original, individual characteristics. But what they gained in
interest, they lost in credibility. Paradoxically, the genre that had
begun as the most realistic, the closest to life, became the most artificial, the furthest removed from life.

Ernest Tidyman (1928–84) produced in John Shaft, who operates
in New York, one of the first black private eyes (*Shaft*, 1970); J. F.
Burke's Sam Kelly (*Death Trick*, 1975) is another. Albert Samson,
who appears in novels by Michael Z. Lewin (b. 1942), is probably
the first fictional detective to operate in Indianapolis, and his name
suggests a certain irony on the part of the author (*Ask the Right
Question*, 1971). Other writers have followed Lewin into the pro-
vinces. Jonathan Valin's (b. 1948) Harry Stonor works in Cincinnati

(*The Lime Pit*, 1980), Loren Estleman's (b. 1952) Amos Walker in Detroit (*Motor City Blue*, 1980), Howard Engel's (b. 1931) Benny Cooperman in Grantham, on the American side of Niagara Falls (*Murder on Location*, 1982), and Michael Allegretto's Jacob Lomax, another ex-cop turned private eye, in Denver (*Death on the Rocks*, 1987). Finally, to match the two English female private detectives Cordelia Gray and Anna Lee, we have two American female private eyes: Sue Grafton's (b. 1940) Kinsey Millhone from Santa Teresa, California ('*A*' *is for Alibi*, 1982), and Sara Paretsky's Vic Warshawski, a policeman's daughter who lives and works in Chicago (*Indemnity Only*, 1982).

MISFITS

There are a few characters who cannot be classified as either private detectives or private eyes. Yet they undoubtedly perform the function of a detective in the books in which they appear.

The most original among them is Gimiendo Hernandez Quinto, a gigantic Mexican who appears in *Murder, Chop Chop* (1942) and two other novels by James Norman (pseudonym of James Norman Schmidt, b. 1912), all of which are set in China at the beginning of the Second World War. Quinto, who is supposed to be a cousin of Pancho Villa, is in command of a detachment of guerrillas whom he is training to fight the Japanese. But in each novel he has a crime to solve, which he does in classical fashion. Travis McGee, hero of a long series of novels by John D. MacDonald (1916–86), the first being *The Deep Blue Good-By* (1964), lives on a houseboat in Fort Lauderdale, Florida. Calling himself a 'salvage consultant', he recovers stolen property for a percentage fee. Like Marlowe, he sees himself— though with some element of self-parody—as a knight-at-arms; but whereas the private eye usually operates in one city only, McGee goes much further afield—to California, Mexico, and Pago-Pago. Philip St Ives, who appears in books by Oliver Bleeck (pseudonym of Ross Thomas, b. 1926), has a similar occupation: he is a professional go-between, paid to ransom stolen property and kidnap victims (*The Brass Go-Between*, 1969). Joe Gores, who has been a private investigator himself, uses a San Francisco firm of auto repossessors, Dan Kearney Associates, as detectives in a series of novels commencing with *Dead Skip* (1972); and James Ellroy (b. 1948) gives his detective Fritz Brown the same job in *Brown's Requiem* (1981).

Chapter 3

THE AMATEUR AMATEUR

He looked Vance up and down. 'Tobacco expert?' he asked, with ill-
disguised sarcasm.
'Oh, dear, no.' Vance's voice was dulcet. 'My speciality is scarab-
cartouches of the Ptolomaic dynasties.'
(S. S. Van Dine, *The Benson Murder Case*)

THE AMATEUR PREDICAMENT

The writer who creates an amateur detective and uses the character in
a series of novels faces much greater difficulties, as far as plausibility
and verisimilitude are concerned, than the author whose series character is a policeman or private detective. For, while the amateur
detective may, with reasonable credibility, become involved in the
investigation of a single crime, credulity is strained beyond breaking-
point if he or she is constantly and conveniently found among those
present when a murder has been committed. In other words, this type
of detective story is the most artificial and contrived of all, and consequently its plots tend to be equally artificial and contrived. Murders
are committed not from the normal motives of lust, greed, or fear, it
often seems, but solely to provide the detective with a baffling problem. At the extreme, exemplified by S. S. Van Dine, Ellery Queen,
and John Dickson Carr, the books lose narrative interest and become
pure intellectual puzzles, with situations which, as Nicholas Blake
wrote of John Dickson Carr, 'possess the mad logic and extravagance
of a dream'.

A further artificiality stems from the fact that the amateur
detective enjoys no *locus standi*, has no authority to question suspects,
no technical knowledge or resources, and is usually impelled by nothing more than insatiable curiosity. It follows that, in order to remain
in touch with the progress of the investigation, he must establish such
a close, unlikely relationship with the official investigator as to be

privy to all the latter's discoveries. This relationship is taken to its ludicrous—if logical—extreme in the Ellery Queen stories, in which the investigating policeman is the amateur's father. Dorothy Sayers does not go quite so far when she gives Lord Peter Wimsey merely a brother-in-law who is a policeman. Establishment of a close relationship with the police does have one advantage, however. It allows the author to skip lightly over the boring routine of an investigation: the checking of alibis, lifting of fingerprints, comparison of bullets, and so on. This can be left to the efficiency of Scotland Yard or the New York Police Department, while the amateur reserves the more interesting, esoteric aspects of the enquiry for himself. Dorothy Sayers expresses this aspect of the relationship neatly in *Whose Body?* (1923), when Lord Peter Wimsey facetiously addresses Inspector Parker—at this time not yet married to his sister—thus: ' "It affords me, if I may say so, the greatest satisfaction," continued the noble lord, "that in a collaboration like ours all the uninteresting and disagreeable routine work is done by you." ' And G. D. H. and M. Cole make the same point when they write in *Death in the Quarry* (1934): 'Everard Blatchington . . . had only the interest of an amateur in crime, and of a dilettante amateur at that. He would never have gone through one tenth of the routine labour necessary to solve an entire case.'

To begin with, a few authors avoided the dangers inherent in the use of an amateur detective by following in the footsteps of Poe, specifically by imitating the method he used in 'The Mystery of Marie Rogêt'. In this story Dupin remains at a distance from the crime throughout. He arrives at a solution solely by considering and analysing newspaper reports of the mystery, acting as pure intellect, as it were. Indeed, Poe intended the story as a tribute not only to Dupin's powers of ratiocination, but also to his own, for in it he endeavoured to solve an actual case, the death in New York of a cigar-store girl called Mary Rogers. He merely transferred the case to Paris, and altered the names of the newspapers. Critics have pointed out, however, that he cheated by adding or subtracting facts to suit his solution and, as it became increasingly apparent that the girl had not been murdered but was the victim of a botched attempt at abortion, subtly altering elements of the story so that, when it appeared in book form two years after its first publication, Poe's conclusions seemed to have been entirely correct from the start.

M. P. Shiel's (1865–1947) Prince Zaleski (*Prince Zaleski*, 1895) is a character very much in the mould of one of Poe's Gothic heroes. A

Russian nobleman, 'victim of a too importunate, too unfortunate Love, which the fulgor of the throne itself could not abash', he has fled his native land and become a voluntary exile from mankind. He lives in England, in a 'vast palace of the older world standing lonely in the midst of woodland, and approached by a sombre avenue of poplars and cypresses, through which the sunlight hardly passed'— the rhythm of the sentence is entirely that of Poe—attended only by a single black servant. Most of the palace is in ruins, inhabited by 'fat and otiose rats'. Zaleski's chamber, hidden in the recesses of the building, is full of curios and *objets d'art*, including a mummy from which the wrappings have been torn, revealing the withered, hideous corpse within. When the narrator—Shiel himself—arrives, Zaleski, who has been indulging himself with hashish, rises to greet him, 'discarding his gemmed chibouque and an old vellum reprint of Anacreon'. Shiel has brought with him a collection of newspaper clippings describing the mysterious death of Lord Pharanx; he reads them to Zaleski, who immediately deduces that the supposed murder is a case of suicide. Two similar short stories complete the volume, which has a fitting epigraph from the prophet Isaiah: 'Come now, and let us reason together'. However incredible Zaleski, the most bizarre of detectives, might be, his procedures and, above all, his relationship to the crime remain perfectly plausible.

The same can be said of Baroness Orczy's Old Man in the Corner, who appeared in a series of magazine stories starting in 1901, later collected in *The Old Man in the Corner* (1909; US title *The Man in the Corner*). He is a pale, thin man who fidgets incessantly with a long piece of string, 'tying and untying it into knots of wonderful and complicated proportions'. In the first story he accosts Polly Burton of the *Evening Observer* as she sits over coffee, a roll, and a plate of tongue in the Norfolk Street branch of the Aerated Bread Company. He tells her that 'there is no such thing as a mystery in connection with any crime, provided intelligence is brought to bear on its investigation', and to prove it, proceeds to solve the latest sensational crime, basing his deductions solely on newspaper reports. Succeeding stories follow the same model. The meeting-place is always the same, and the old man, having obtained all his material from accounts in the Press, though he occasionally visits the scene of a crime or attends an inquest, solves the case for Polly, tying knots the while—a habit of which she cleverly succeeds in breaking him in the last story. The stories are generally neat and well thought out, shorter and closer to the Conan Doyle model than the later Skin o' my Tooth stories described in the previous chapter.

However, theoretical ratiocination had its limits. The detective could not remain a hermit for ever; he had to emerge from his isolation to become part of the action, to mingle and converse with the suspects, even to be threatened and attacked by the criminal at times. Like their more professional colleagues, these new amateur detectives fall naturally into a number of sub-groups. It is surprising, however, how few these sub-groups are, and how much the detectives resemble one another, given that there is no particular reason for the amateur detective, unlike his professional counterpart, to follow one career rather than another.

ACADEMICS

Academics form by far the largest group of amateur detectives. This is no doubt partly due to the fact that many of the authors themselves come from the academic world, and partly to the baseless assumption that deductive acumen and scholarly eminence go hand in hand. The earliest example is Professor S. F. X. Van Dusen, who appears in a number of stories by Jacques Futrelle (1875–1912)—the first are collected in *The Thinking Machine* (1907; also published as *The Problem of Cell 13*)—set in an unnamed American city. The professor is a comic caricature of a scholar; thin, pale, and stooped, he wears immensely thick glasses, and has a forehead 'almost abnormal in its height and width'. He has been called 'The Thinking Machine' after a remarkable chess match in which he demonstrated that 'a stranger to the game might, by the force of inevitable logic, defeat a champion who had devoted a life-time to its study'. He made his début in a much anthologized story, 'The Problem of Cell 13', first published in a Boston newspaper in 1905. In it he accepts an after-dinner challenge from two of his friends that he cannot escape from the condemned cell in the city's prison, and, of course, succeeds in doing so without difficulty. But the story is disappointing as a demonstration of the power of the intellect, since the escape depends upon a unique peculiarity of the cell's construction—a disused drain-pipe which communicates with the outside world—and is achieved only with outside help. On the whole the stories are very similar to, though less convincing than, Arthur B. Reeve's Craig Kennedy stories.

The next academic detective, John Rhode's (pseudonym of Cecil

John Charles Street, 1884–1965) Dr Priestley, appears after a lengthy gap in *The Paddington Mystery* (1925). Unlike Futrelle, who never makes it clear to what particular branch of science Van Dusen owes allegiance, Rhode immediately tells us that Priestley is 'cursed with a restless brain and an almost immoral passion for mathematics'. Indeed, he claims to have forestalled Einstein, and to have been the first 'to breach the citadel of Newton'. In his long career, which spans nearly forty years and some seventy books, Priestley undergoes some interesting metamorphoses. On his introduction, when he clears up the affairs of a young man called Harold Merefield, who later becomes his secretary, he performs almost completely in a ratiocinative capacity, undertaking little or no investigation himself. The Priestley of the middle period, however, is far more active: assisted by Merefield, he conducts investigations, searches for clues, and on several occasions only just escapes death at the hands of the criminal. Later he reverts to his earlier behaviour, becoming a testy oracle who, from an armchair in his study in Westbourne Terrace, offers Delphic advice to Superintendent Hanslet and Inspector Jimmy Waghorn when they come to him for help with their most difficult cases. Though a less impressive and less polymathically learned figure than Dr Thorndyke, Priestley is very reminiscent of Freeman's hero. Certainly when he tells Merefield that 'the trained mind, . . . that is to say, the brain accustomed to logical reasoning processes, can often construct an edifice of unshakable truth from the loose bricks of fact which to others seem merely a profitless rubbish heap', the idea has a very Thorndykian ring, though his injunction, 'Tell me your procedure, omitting no detail, however apparently irrelevant', is an obvious echo of one of Sherlock Holmes's most famous remarks.

After Priestley the curious view—implicit in both Futrelle's stories and Rhode's early books—that logic is the prerogative of the scientist's lapses; and in the course of the ensuing years few university departments remain unrepresented by an academic detective.

Henry Poggioli, Ph.D., the Italian-American hero of a number of short stories by T. S. Stribling (1881–1965) (*Clues of the Caribbees*, 1929), a 'smallish dark-eyed gentleman of a certain academic appearance', is an instructor in psychology at Ohio State University. But the stories all take place in the West Indies, a setting which gives them a certain charm, where Poggioli is travelling while on sabbatical leave. His efforts to solve the mysteries he encounters are not always successful, and his professional expertise is hardly employed.

An Oxford Tragedy (1933) by J.C. Masterman (1891–1977), later provost of Worcester College, is possibly the best of the many detective stories set in Oxford. Though it is narrated by Francis Winn, vice-president and senior tutor of St Thomas's College, the detective to whom he acts as Watson is not an Oxford academic but a Viennese lawyer and visiting lecturer, Ernst Brendel, who both detects and discourses on detection with admirable sense. His presence allows the internal view of Oxford to be corrected by an external one, thus avoiding the descent into sentimentality which can affect accounts of college life. A very similar character, who is used in the same way to cast a mildly critical eye on English tradition, is Dr Wenceslaus Bottwink, sometime professor of modern history in the University of Prague. A specialist in eighteenth-century English political history, he uses his knowledge of the English constitution to solve the crime in *An English Murder* (1951; US title *The Christmas Murder*) by Cyril Hare (pseudonym of Alfred Alexander Gordon Clark, 1900–58), whose other detectives, the lawyer Pettigrew and the policeman Mallett, are discussed below. Though short, *An English Murder* is one of Hare's best works, and is an exceedingly good detective story in the classical mould. The murder takes place at Christmas in an English stately home isolated by a heavy snowfall, and has what is possibly a unique motive for the crime.

Anthony Boucher's private detective Fergus O'Breen has been noted above; the *New York Times* critic of detective fiction also produced a rather more successful amateur armchair detective in *The Case of the Seven of Calvary* (1937). This is Dr Ashwin, professor of Sanskrit at the University of California, a large man with a taste for beer, bourbon, and detective novels. He is based on the professor of Sanskrit at Berkeley, Arthur William Ryder, to whom the novel is dedicated.

Charlotte Armstrong's (1905–69) MacDougal Duff (*Lay On, Mac Duff!*, 1942) has a claim to be considered a private detective. A tall, lean man with a melancholy, seamed face, he is a professor of American history, who, as a hobby, solves mysteries from the accounts given in newspapers, finds that he can make money by doing this, and therefore retires. As detection, the novels in which he features are not wholly satisfactory.

One of the most successful academic detectives is Gervase Fen, professor of English Language and Literature in the University of Oxford, who appears in a number of novels and short stories by

Edmund Crispin (pseudonym of Robert Bruce Montgomery, 1921–78), the first of which is *The Case of the Gilded Fly* (1944; US title *Obsequies at Oxford*). Fen is tall and thin, with a ruddy, clean-shaven face and dark hair plastered down with water which breaks out 'into disaffected fragments towards the crown'. He wears rain-coats that are too large for him, and his hats are extraordinary. In some respects he is supposed to have been modelled on Will Moore, tutor in French at St John's College, where Crispin was an under-graduate. Crispin is always amusing, and can be very funny, while Fen, who claims to be 'the only literary critic turned detective in the whole of fiction', is capable of very workmanlike—sometimes even brilliant—feats of detection. But his whimsicalities and eccentricities can be tedious and exasperating, and there is often too much by-play with his wayward little car, Lily Christine. The better novels are probably those which do not take place in Oxford.

Peter Shane, the detective in books (*Dead Reckoning*, 1943) by Francis Bonnamy (pseudonym of Audrey Walz), is again almost a professional, since crime is his livelihood. He is an academic criminologist at the University of Chicago, and Bonnamy is his pro-fessional colleague, his assistant, and his chronicler. Putting the author into the story in this manner is a somewhat naïve device for adding verisimilitude to an otherwise unconvincing narrative, but it has nevertheless commended itself to a number of detective novelists. M. P. Shiel, using his own name, visits Prince Zaleski in his eremitic retreat. S. S. Van Dine represents himself as a lawyer who looks after Philo Vance's financial affairs and narrates his client's investigations of murders in New York. Ellery Queen and Tod Claymore both write of their own cases, one in the third person, the other in the first.

Glyn Daniel (1914–86), an archaeologist and fellow of St John's College, Cambridge, has produced an archaeologist-detective from Cambridge in the character of Sir Richard Cherrington, vice-president of Fisher College and professor of prehistory in the univer-sity (*The Cambridge Murders*, 1945; originally published under the pseudonym Dilwyn Rees). Cherrington does a reasonable job as a detective, and is also convincing as an archaeologist and college offi-cer. Another archaeologist-detective is the one-handed—he has left the other under a thorn-bush in a wadi near the Mareth Line—Martin Cotterell, who appears in a number of novels by John Trench (b. 1920). Extremely well written, the books are perhaps somewhat over-plotted; but Cotterell himself is a strong, attractive character who cracks an archaeological code in the first novel, *Docken Dead* (1953), the story of a search for a lost sixth-century British chronicle.

Bodies in a Bookshop (1946) is one of a number of novels in which the amateur detective is the pipe-smoking, beer-drinking, Scottish professor of botany John Stubbs. The detection is poor, and the cross-talk between Stubbs and the policeman, Chief Inspector Reginald Bishop, unamusing. Indeed, the book would not be worth mentioning were it not for the fact that the author, here named R. T. Campbell, is in fact the Scottish poet Ruthven Campbell Todd (1914–78).

Timothy Fuller (b. 1914) has written a series of lively and amusing novels—in all of which a great deal of liquor is consumed—about Jupiter Jones, who, when we first meet him in *Harvard has a Homicide* (1936; UK title *J for Jupiter*) is a graduate student in the Fine Arts department at Harvard, but in succeeding novels becomes first an instructor and then an assistant professor in the same department.

Professor Mandrake is a large, strikingly ugly, excessively untidy anthropologist who appears in several English detective stories by John and Emery Bonett (pseudonyms of John Hubert Arthur Coulson, b. 1906, and Felicity Winifred Carter, b. 1906). An amateur criminologist, he has little opportunity for detection, since the mysteries tend to solve themselves (*Dead Lion*, 1949).

Leo Bruce (pseudonym of Rupert Croft-Cooke, 1903–79), whose Sergeant Beef stories are dealt with in the final chapter of the book, also wrote a series of detective novels in which the hero is Carolus Deane, senior history master at the Queen's School, Newminster, and author of *Who Killed William Rufus? And Other Mysteries of History*. Deane, an ex-commando, is slim, dapper, and rather pale, has a large private income, and dresses too well for a schoolmaster. He has a passionate interest in crime, and, like other amateur detectives, practises deduction by solving cases reported in the newspapers. An odious pupil, Rupert Priggley, encourages him to put his theories into practice, and becomes his assistant (*At Death's Door*, 1955).

Although Nuri Izkirlak, Joan Fleming's (1908–80) Turkish philosopher (*When I Grow Rich*, 1962) is not strictly an academic, he creeps in here by virtue of his interests and his passionate desire to visit Oxford. A more genuine Oxford philosopher is Ambrose Usher, fellow of St Mary's College and hero of several novels by Jocelyn Davey (pseudonym of Chaim Raphael, b. 1908). Usher certainly thinks and acts as a philosopher, and much of the pleasure of the novels comes from ruminations on his part which are not particularly relevant to the main intrigue. He is said to be a portrait of Isaiah Berlin, who was with the author at the British Embassy in Washington during the Second World War. The first novel, *The Undoubted Deed* (1956; US title *A Capitol Offence*)—the title is a quotation from Melville's *Moby Dick*—uses the diplomatic circles of Washington as its setting, but takes place after the war.

Adam Ludlow, hero of novels by Simon Nash (pseudonym of Raymond Chapman, b. 1924), a tall, thin man in his forties with deep grey eyes under rugged brows, is a lecturer in English at the North London College. He might have become a brilliant academic, but has been held back by 'the combination of a small private income, a diversity of non-academic interests and a lazy nature'. He therefore welcomes his accidental encounter with crime, in *Dead of a Counterplot* (1962), and turns out to be, both here and in later books, no mean hand with a deduction. Like Gervase Fen, to whom he perhaps owes something, he owns an ancient, wayward car which in a moment of sentimental whimsy he has named Cleopatra, because, of course, 'Age cannot wither her, nor custom stale her infinite variety.'

Another member of an English faculty is Kate Fansler, a professor at an unnamed New York university—presumably Columbia, where her creator, Amanda Cross (pseudonym of Carolyn G. Heilbrun, b. 1926) teaches. Of all the detectives in this group, Professor Fansler is undoubtedly the most convincing academic. And one of the most satisfying qualities of the books in which she appears is the way she brings a scholar's mind to bear on a problem of detection. An assistant district attorney friend remarks disparagingly that, 'As a detective, Kate made an excellent literary critic.' But the laugh is on him, for it is the application of critical techniques that solves the mystery. Amanda Cross has said that she began writing because she could no longer find detective stories which combined conversation with literary mysteries and which treated women as people in their own right, rather than decorative appendages. She has certainly filled the gap: the conversation in her novels is especially enjoyable, often overshadowing the investigation itself. There is an occasional weakness of plot, however; certainly the basic premiss of her first novel, *In the Last Analysis* (1964), is hardly credible.

A Taste of Power (1966) by W. J. Burley (b. 1914) introduces Henry Lancaster Pym, MA, D.Phil., D.Sc., a zoologist who is asked to investigate an epidemic of anonymous letters at a co-educational school. Though he is an effective detective, Pym is yet another character who has too many individual eccentricities, perhaps. The possessor of a large private income, he has retired at the age of 30 and built himself a house in a remote Cornish village, where he carries on his zoological research assisted by an attractive blonde secretary and a super-efficient factotum.

A much easier character to swallow is Dr R. V. Davie, the elderly—he is in his seventies—emeritus fellow of St Nicholas's College, Cambridge, who appears in *Death's Bright Dart* (1967) and other novels by V. C. Clinton-Baddeley (1900–70). Dr Davie may be the oldest fictional detective, but his mind is as keen as that of many half his age. At the same time he claims the privileges of his years, and a good deal of the charm of the novels comes from the way in which they view the world through an elderly consciousness.

Another Oxford English don, in the tradition of Gervase Fen though rather less eccentric, is Patrick Grant, fellow and dean of St Mark's College, 'a tall, well-built man with thick straight dark hair and a pair of very keen hazel eyes', who is the detective in *Dead in the Morning* (1970) and other novels by Margaret Yorke (pseudonym of Margaret Nicholson, b. 1924).

The last member of this group returns us in pleasing fashion to the first. S. F. X. Dean (pseudonym of Francis Smith) has written several novels—*By Frequent Anguish* (1982) is the first—in which the hero-detective is Neil Kelly, a middle-aged professor of English at Old Hampton College in New England. The author's *nom de plume* was presumably adopted in homage to Professor S. F. X. Van Dusen, the Thinking Machine.

PHILIP TRENT

It is not easy to find a single designation for the second most numerous category of amateur detectives. Once characterized, however, the type is easily recognizable. The detective, English or American, is always male and usually a member of the upper classes. If he is not a collector or connoisseur with a large private income, he is probably an artist or author. More often than not he is a bachelor, and frequently he has a manservant with whom he enjoys something of the same kind of relationship as that which unites P. G. Wodehouse's Bertie Wooster and Jeeves. He is usually as amiable—and occasionally appears as foolish—as Wooster; but the foolishness is only a mask, concealing a keen brain and an iron will. His most distinguishing characteristic, however, is his mode of speech, which consists almost entirely of facetious banter heavily spiced with quotations—often mangled—from English literature.

The first example of this species was provided by E. C. Bentley (1875–1956) in *Trent's Last Case* (1912; original US title *The Woman in Black*). Philip Trent is an artist who, when the millionaire Sigsbee Manderson is murdered, is somewhat surprisingly asked by a newspaper editor to investigate the crime. Trent is young, long and loosely-built, with a 'high-boned, quixotic face' and short moustache, and is usually untidily dressed and uncombed. He fits closely the model presented above; and his manner of speech is particularly paradigmatic, as the following exchange, with its humorous misquotation of Byron, indicates:

'The wine here', Trent resumed, as they seated themselves, 'is almost certainly made out of grapes. What shall we drink?'

Mr Cupples came out of his reverie. 'I think', he said, 'I will have milk and soda water.'

'Speak lower!' urged Trent. 'The head-waiter has a weak heart, and might hear you. Milk and soda water! Cupples, you may think you have a strong constitution, and I don't say you have not, but I warn you that this habit of mixing drinks has been the death of many a robuster man than you. Be wise in time. Fill high the cup with Samian wine, leave soda to the Turkish hordes.'

In his autobiography *Those Days* (1940) Bentley gives an account of how he came to write the novel. He wished to write a detective story of a new sort, he says, a 'detective story in which the detective was recognizable as a human being, and was not quite so much the "heavy" sleuth'. He resolved to make the detective fall in love with the murdered man's widow, which he felt to be a 'supremely absurd' idea, adding that the most pleasing notion of all was that of 'making the hero's hard-won and obviously correct solution to the mystery turn out to be completely wrong. . . . The triumphantly incriminated suspect should prove to be innocent after all, and a cleverer fellow than the hero.' He concludes by pointing out that *Trent's Last Case* is 'not so much a detective story as an exposure of detective stories', and expresses surprise that this has not been more generally noticed. In fact it is an exposure not so much of the detective story as of the detective. Bentley has broken the image of the infallible, omniscient, inhumanly unsusceptible great detective, and given detection a more human face. Trent is proved resoundingly wrong twice, is far from omniscient, and falls violently in love with the chief suspect. Indeed, he is so cast down by his failure that he vows never to touch a crime mystery again: the Manderson affair will be Philip Trent's last case, he announces. Luckily Bentley did not take him at his word; he followed the book with a number of excellent short stories and another novel, all of which have Trent as their detective.

Bentley's work has wit, style, and panache. Trent is genuinely amusing, and his *badinage* stems from an irresistible flow of high spirits. Unfortunately, the same cannot always be said of his successors, in whose hands the conversational idiom often degenerates into heavy facetiousness or fatuous whimsy, not infrequently laced with an offputting snobbishness.

Lee Thayer (Emma Redington Thayer, née Lee, 1874–1973) wrote some sixty novels—the last was published when she was 92—about a New York man-about-town Peter Clancy. Clancy is a private detective, so strictly speaking belongs in the previous chapter, but he fits the amateur gentleman image too well not to be included here. He has a fastidious English valet, Wiggar, who often finds it necessary to correct his employer on minutiae of etiquette or dress. The relationship between the two is amusing, and the books are pleasant and unassuming (*The Mystery of the 13th Floor*, 1919).

The best-known example of this type, however, must be Lord Peter Wimsey, who appears in eleven novels and a number of short stories by Dorothy Sayers (1893–1957), beginning with *Whose Body?* (1923). In creating Wimsey, Sayers learnt from the mistakes of her predecessors. She began by giving him a definite history, first encapsulated in the fake extract from Debrett that precedes the narrative in the early novels, later expanded into a six-page biographical note ostensibly written by Wimsey's uncle, Paul Delagardie. In this way she was able, unlike Conan Doyle or Freeman, to avoid contradictions and inconsistencies in Wimsey's biography in the course of the books. At the same time she did not fall into the trap in which Agatha Christie had been caught a few years earlier: she gave Wimsey no real eccentricities other than those suited to the fictional embodiment of his class and kind. He may be a better cricketer or have a keener brain than most; but otherwise he is indistinguishable from a multitude of aristocratic heroes in novels, plays, and films of the period. Younger brother of the Duke of Denver, Wimsey lives in a modern flat at 110A Piccadilly, attended by Bunter, his sergeant during the war and now his manservant and assistant in the investigation of crime. His policeman-friend is Charles Parker of Scotland Yard, who later marries Wimsey's sister Mary. With no pretensions to good looks, Wimsey has 'a long, narrow chin, and a long, receding forehead, accentuated by the brushed-back sleekness of his tow-coloured hair'. In a memorable image, his face is described as looking 'as if it had generated spontaneously from his top hat, as white maggots breed from Gorgonzola'. Though Wimsey is always worthy of respect as a detective, Sayers rather overdoes the silly ass aspect of his character in the early novels, making him into a kind of fatuous buffoon. Nor are her attempts to establish him as a connoisseur of food, drink, and incunabula always convincing. He tells Parker to get Bunter to give him 'a bottle of the Chateau Yquem—it's rather decent', as if this lusciously sweet white wine, the best of all Sauternes, were something that could be drunk with just any food. Equally unconvincing are his acrobatics, dressed as a harlequin, in *Murder Must Advertise* (1933), where the author appears to be trying to turn him into a more conventional Romantic hero. In the later novels the fatuousness is toned down, however, and Wimsey becomes a more serious and a more interesting character. In *Strong Poison* (1930) he falls in love with Harriet Vane, who has been falsely accused of murder, and after a long courtship marries her at the beginning of *Busman's Honeymoon* (1937). Harriet is a detective story writer; it is tempting to see her as Dorothy Sayers's *alter ego*, through whom she is able to enjoy vicariously a love-affair with her hero. Not only Wimsey, but the novels themselves become more serious with time, culminating in *Gaudy Night* (1935), which treats, in subtle and interesting fashion, the problems of women's education and the role of women in society.

Roger Sheringham, the detective in a number of pleasant novels by Anthony Berkeley (pseudonym of Anthony Berkeley Cox, 1893–1971), is very much in the mould of Trent. He is an author, smokes a large pipe, was educated at Winchester and Oxford, and has a gift for reasonably amusing persiflage. Like Bentley, Berkeley believes the detective should be human. In the dedication to the first Sheringham book, *The Layton Court Mystery* (1925), addressed to his father, he writes:

You will notice that I have tried to make the gentleman who eventually solves the mystery behave as nearly as possible as he might be expected to behave in real life. That is to say, he is very far removed from a sphinx, and he does make a mistake or two occasionally. . . . I cannot see why even a detective story should not aim at the creation of a natural atmosphere, just as much as any other work of the lighter fiction.

Herbert Adams (1874–1952) wrote a number of novels in which the detective is Roger Bennion, a dark, clean-shaven man in his thirties who works with his father, Sir Christopher Bennion, as a property developer. During the Second World War he becomes an intelligence officer. The books are pleasant, if slow-moving. Adams was a keen golfer, and several of the novels have a golfing background—for example, *Death off the Fairway* (1936).

The American equivalent of Lord Peter Wimsey is Philo Vance, who appears in twelve novels by S. S. Van Dine (pseudonym of Willard Huntington Wright, 1888–1939)—the first is *The Benson Murder Case* (1926). Wright was a distinguished art critic who had studied in Paris and Munich. During a two-year convalescence following a breakdown, he read over 2,000 detective stories and excogitated a theory of detective fiction—namely, that 'the detective story is a kind of intellectual game . . . a sporting event'—which he proceeded to put into practice in his novels. Set in New York, these purport to be narrated by Van Dine, Vance's friend, admirer, and lawyer. Vance himself, whose name, we are told, is a pseudonym, is 'an aristocrat by birth and instinct', unusually good-looking, though his mouth is 'ascetic and cruel'. He has a full, sloping forehead, widely spaced grey eyes, and a narrow prominent chin with a deep cleft. An Englishman, Currie, serves as his butler, valet, major-domo, and, occasionally, cook. Vance is an authority on art, a connoisseur with a very varied collection of treasures, which include

a black-figured amphora by Amasis, a proto-Corinthian vase in the Aegean style, Koubatcha and Rodian plates, Athenian pottery, a sixteenth-century Italian holy-water stoup of rock crystal, pewter of the Tudor period . . ., a bronze plaque by Cellini, a triptych of Limoges enamel, a Spanish retable of an altar-piece by Vallfogona, several Etruscan bronzes, an Indian Greco Buddhist, a statuette of the Goddess Kuan Yin from the Ming dynasty, a number of very fine Renaissance wood-cuts and several specimens of Byzantine, Carolingian and early French ivory carvings.

He has an affected English accent—like Reggie Fortune, he regularly elides his final g's—and his normal conversational manner is marked by languid sarcasm, as in the remark which forms the epigraph to this chapter. Unlike most other detectives, Vance does not depend on evidence to reach his conclusions. 'The material indications of the crime don't enter into my calculations, y'know—I leave 'em entirely to you lawyers and the lads with the bulging deltoids', he says. His method is psychological: just as one can tell the identity of an artist from the brush-strokes on a canvas, so one can tell a murderer by the congruence between his psychological profile and the way in which the crime has been committed. In *The Canary Murder Case* (1927) Vance plays poker with the suspects in order to deduce their character from the way in which they bet and bluff. Vance's mannerisms, his affectations, and his knowingness soon become irritating; and, though the first two books are based on actual murder cases (the Joseph Browne Elwell case and the 'Dot' King case) and are thus reasonably realistic, succeeding plots become more and more bizarre. In *The Bishop Murder Case* (1929) the murders are based on nursery rhymes, and Vance often has little to do as the suspects are eliminated one after another, leaving one sole survivor who must be the murderer.

Another aristocrat is the Honourable Everard Blatchington, heir to Lord Blatchington, the amateur detective in novels (*The Blatchington Tangle*, 1926) by G. D. H. (1889–1959) and M. Cole (1893–1980). Like Wimsey, Blatchington leaves the difficult and routine work of an enquiry to a policeman, Superintendent Wilson, who appears on his own in other stories by the authors.

Even more aristocratic is Margery Allingham's (1904–66) Albert Campion, who first appears in *Crime at Black Dudley* (1929; US title *The Black Dudley Murder*). He has royal connections, and may even be an heir to the throne. Campion is of course a pseudonym; his real surname is too eminent to be mentioned, though we learn that his first name is in reality not Albert but Rudolph. Not unlike Wimsey physically—he is described as 'the fresh-faced young man with the tow-coloured hair and the foolish, pale-blue eyes behind tortoiseshell-rimmed spectacles'—he appears even more fatuous and asinine—even lunatic—in his behaviour and conversation, using this apparent foolishness to dupe his opponents. His manservant is quite unlike Bunter, however. Magersfontein Lugg is a reformed burglar, whom Campion once described as having 'the courage of his previous convictions'. Lugg is not as amusing a character as his author believed him to be, though; and the best books are probably those in which he plays little or no part. The friend and collaborator in the police force so necessary to the amateur detective is supplied first by Stanislaus Oates and, following his retirement, by his protégé Charlie Luke, a large, superabundantly energetic Cockney. Like Wimsey, Campion grows more serious and more sensible with time, especially after his marriage to aircraft engineer Amanda Fitton, whom he first meets in *Sweet Danger* (1933; US title *Kingdom of Death*; also in US as *The Fear Sign*) but does not marry until after *Traitor's Purse* (1941; US title *The Sabotage Murder Mystery*). Margery Allingham's work is less realistic than that of Dorothy Sayers. She delights in creating wild, outré settings and peopling them with eccentric, odd characters. Moreover, she has a weakness for melodrama; and the criminal gang, eschewed by most serious writers of detective fiction, makes an occasional appearance in her novels. Her method also differs from that of her colleague. If Wimsey is always the central figure in the cases in which he is involved, the same cannot be said of Campion, who often seems to adopt the role of a bystander, the mystery being viewed through other eyes. Were Wimsey removed from the novels of Dorothy Sayers, they would collapse; the removal of Campion from the work of Margery Allingham would not be altogether disastrous, by contrast.

Christopher Bush (1888–1973) wrote some eighty novels, in all of which the detective is Ludovic Travers, a rich bachelor who is the nephew of a commissioner at Scotland Yard; the connection gives Travers an entrée to cases investigated by Bush's policeman, Superintendent Wharton. (*The Plumley Inheritance*, 1926).

If S. S. Van Dine is both author and Vance's Watson, Ellery Queen (pseudonym of Frederic Dannay, 1905–82, and Manfred B. Lee, 1905–71) is both author and detective, writing, rather oddly, of his own exploits in the third person. The first Ellery Queen novel, *The Roman Hat Mystery* (1929), was complicated by an extra piece of rusty narrative machinery: the book purported to be presented to the public by one J. J. McC., who has visited Ellery in Italy, where he is living in retirement with his wife, child, and father, and persuaded him to disgorge an account of one of his most famous cases. In subsequent novels this device is dropped, and Ellery's wife and child are silently forgotten. Ellery is tall, young, and looks athletic, although he sports a rimless pince-nez. He is a writer of detective stories who lives with his father, Inspector Richard Queen of the New York police, in an apartment of West 87th Street, where they are looked after by Djuna, a 19-year-old orphan of indeterminate race. The relationship between detective and reader is a new one in the early Ellery Queen books, making them into something approaching Van

Dine's 'intellectual game'. In Doyle's books the reader cannot pre-empt Holmes's deductions, for the evidence on which they are based—the tattoo of a fish with its scales stained a delicate pink, which must have been executed by a Chinese tattooist, for example—is usually displayed only after the deductions have been made. And if we are shown the evidence at the same time as Thorndyke in the novels of Freeman, we are often unable to draw the correct conclusion from it, since we probably do not have the requisite knowledge—we do not know the difference between greater and lesser duckweed, for example. Queen, by contrast, plays with impeccable fairness: in each of the first eleven books the narrative stops after all the necessary facts have been presented. Readers are then invited to solve the mystery for themselves, and in each case there is a perfectly logical solution. Nevertheless, this is achieved only at some cost; for although the solution may be logically deducible, it is always complex and highly artificial. In *The Roman Hat Mystery* we are constrained to believe in a blackmailer who keeps the papers relating to each of his victims tucked inside a different hat, with the victim's name indelibly marked on the inner lining. The hats are then concealed in a hidden cupboard built into the ceiling above his bed. With ratiocination at a premium, character portrayal, narrative tension, and other novelistic qualities fly out of the window; nor are the gruesomely jocular exchanges between Ellery and his father adequate compensation. These are undoubtedly the most artificial of all detective stories, with all the excitement and romantic attraction of a crossword puzzle.

With Ellery Queen the Philip Trent tradition begins to draw to a close, though a few more examples can be noted. Cecil John Street, whose stories written under the name of John Rhode have already been discussed, also produced a series of novels using the pseudonym Miles Burton, in which the detective is Desmond Merrion. Merrion is a man of independent and very considerable means, 'a living encyclopaedia on all manner of obscure subjects which the ordinary person knows nothing about'. A bachelor at the beginning of the first novel in which he appears, *The Secret of High Eldersham* (1930; also as *The Mystery of High Eldersham*), he meets and marries his wife during the course of it, rescuing her, with the help of his valet Newport, from a sect of Satan-worshippers. During the war, like a number of other fictional detectives and policemen, including Herbert Adams's Roger Bennion, he finds a natural niche in Intelligence.

Malcolm Warren, a young but valetudinarian stockbroker, acts as the narrator-detective in several excellent, charmingly written novels by C. H. B. Kitchin (1895–1967)—*Death of My Aunt* (1930) is the first. Finally, James Hilton (1900–54), author of *Lost Horizon* and *Goodbye, Mr Chips*, wrote one extremely good detective story, *Was It Murder?* (1931; originally published as *Murder at School* by Glen Trevor). The hero, Colin Revell, is a young man who has recently come down from Oxford and is living a somewhat Bohemian life in London while trying to write a full-length satirical epic—a number of stanzas from which are quoted in the narrative—in the manner of Byron's *Don Juan*. Like Trent, Revell falls in love in the course of his investigations—he has been asked by the headmaster of his old school to look into a suspicious accident—and, like Trent, turns out to be completely wrong in his conclusions.

This type of detective is very much a product of the 1920s and 1930s, and since then no new examples have appeared. Some figures, such as Ellery Queen and Desmond Merrion, both heroes of a long series of books, continued through the war and afterwards, but in so doing they lost just those characteristics which identified them with the type. Among the remaining amateur detectives a few sub-groups can be identified: priests, actors and other theatrical personages, husband and wife teams, and bankers. A heterogeneous majority, however, must be lumped together under the two uninformative headings of miscellaneous female and miscellaneous male.

PRIESTS, MISSIONARIES, AND RABBIS

Almost as well known as Sherlock Holmes or Hercule Poirot is Father Brown, the short, dumpy Roman Catholic priest from Essex, with his black hat, large shabby umbrella, and collection of brown paper parcels, about whom G. K. Chesterton (1874–1936) wrote a number of short stories—*The Innocence of Father Brown* (1911) is the first collection. Their hero is based on a friend of Chesterton's, Father John O'Connor, parish priest of St Cuthbert's, Bradford. Father Brown's method of detection is empathetic: he thinks himself into the mind of the criminal, aided by the knowledge of crime and criminal methods gained by listening to the confessions of his parishioners. 'Has it never struck you', he asks in 'The Blue Cross', the first story in which he appears, 'that a man who does next to nothing but hear men's real sins is not likely to be wholly unaware of human evil?' The best of the stories are undoubted masterpieces, brilliantly and poetically written, with the plot often turning on an ingenious, original paradox. Yet at the same time they are less satisfactory as detective stories. The premisses are often so fantastic as to render the whole story absurd. In 'The Hammer of God', for example, a murder is committed by dropping a hammer from the top of a church tower on to the head of a man underneath. Setting aside the difficulty of accuracy of aim, given the aerodynamic qualities of the missile, it is obvious that a hammer dropped from a height would descend with the haft perpendicular and would strike with the end, not the face, of the head. A cursory inspection of the wound and the instrument would reveal this, and make the solution of the problem obvious. More important, with Chesterton the detective story form conceals another intent; examined closely, the stories reveal themselves as parables, in which moral theology is presented as detection. This is not to say that the moral content forces itself upon the reader. In fact, Chesterton's skill as a writer manifests itself precisely in the way in which the moral aspects are concealed.

Dr Mary Finney and Emily Collins are not priests, but 'itinerant missionaries, with Miss Collins working the soul-and-hymn department while Miss Finney ministered to the flesh'. They, together with young Hooper Tolliver, the narrator, appear in several interesting and unusual detective novels by Matthew Head (pseudonym of John Canaday, b. 1907), set in or around Brazzaville in the Congo, where the author spent some time on a government mission during the Second World War (*The Devil in the Bush*, 1945).

Father Joseph Bredder, chaplain of the Convent of Holy Innocents in Los Angeles, is the hero of a number of books by Leonard Holton (pseudonym of Leonard Wibberley, 1915–83). A 40-year-old ex-marine, Father Bredder is six foot, one and a half inches tall and weighs two hundred pounds (*The Saint Maker*, 1959). Harry Kemelman (b. 1908) has written a series of novels about David Small, the scholarly young rabbi of Barnard's Crossing, a small town in Massachusetts, who solves mysteries by the application of pilpul, or Talmudic logic. The town's police chief, Hugh Lanigan, a Roman Catholic, is at first suspicious, but gradually becomes a friend, and eventually turns to the rabbi automatically when confronted with a difficult case. The author has written that his purpose is 'to explain— via a fictional setting—the Jewish religion'; and certainly the novels, pleasantly written and ingeniously plotted, do contain a propaedeutic element (*Friday the Rabbi Slept Late*, 1964). The two novels by the poet Ishmael Reed (b. 1938), *Mumbo Jumbo* (1972) and *The Last Days of Louisiana Red* (1974), with their anarchic, fragmented narration and wild surrealistic style, can only loosely be called detective novels; but they do have mysteries to solve and murders to investigate, as well as an amateur detective in the form of the hoo-doo priest PaPa LaBas. More conventional are the stories by William Kienzle (b. 1928), set in Detroit, in which Father Bob Koesler, priest-editor of the *Detroit Catholic*, the diocesan weekly paper, is the detective (*The Rosary Murders*, 1979).

THE THEATRE

The theatre is a popular setting for detective novels: both Ellery Queen and Edmund Crispin chose it as the venue for their first novels. Generally speaking, actors are more colourful and interesting than the normal run of humanity; moreover, a repertory company provides the closed society dear to the heart of the classical detective novelist, and the building of the theatre itself, with its entrances and exits, passages, coulisses, subterranean labyrinths, and galleries and gantries above the stage, offers as many opportunities for mysterious disappearances and appearances as a Gothic castle or a medieval manor. The use of actors as detectives is far less frequent than the use of their habitat, however. The first example seems to be Sir John Saumarez, hero of *Enter Sir John* (1929) and other novels by Clemence Dane (pseudonym of Winifred Ashton, 1887–1965) and Helen Simpson (1897–1940). Sir John, actor-manager of the Sheridan theatre in Shaftesbury Avenue, is close to the Philip Trent model; he is described as 'slim, languid and perfectly tailored . . . with innumerable affectations'. We learn, however, that he has changed his name from Jonathan Simmonds, and originally came from the north of England. The plot of *Enter Sir John* is oddly similar to that of Dorothy Sayers's *Strong Poison* (1930): in both the hero saves a girl who has been tried for murder, by discovering the real criminal. Sir John is allowed to marry the girl at the end of the book, however, and as far as weight, seriousness, and detection go, there is no comparison: Sayers is immeasurably superior, though *Enter Sir John* is light and not unamusing.

Pete Duluth, the amateur detective in several novels by Patrick Quentin (pseudonym of Hugh Callingham Wheeler, b. 1912, and Richard Wilson Webb), is a Broadway producer, who, when we first meet him in *A Puzzle for Fools* (1936), is drying out in a private sanitarium, having become an alcoholic after losing his wife in a theatre fire. By the end of the novel, however, he has acquired a replacement. But there is little detection and even less plausibility. Gypsy Rose Lee (pseudonym of Rosa Louise Hovick, 1914-70), the famous ecdysiast, produced several novels (*The G-String Murders*, 1941), ghost-written by Craig Rice, in which she herself tells the story and plays the detective. The backstage atmosphere is well done, and the technicalities on stripping not without interest.

Glyn Carr (pseudonym of Frank Showell Styles, b. 1908) wrote fifteen novels about actor-manager Abercrombie Lewker before, as he felt, exhausting the vein—the first is *Death on Milestone Buttress* (1951). Lewker, who in the later novels acquires a knighthood, is pompous and portly, with 'jowls worthy of a Roman emperor'. Like many amateur detectives he worked for British Intelligence during the war; he is 'not only a notable actor, but also a notable man of action'. Lewker's profession is of little importance, however, for these pleasant, amusing stories owe their initial conception to the author's interest in rock climbing and mountaineering. Real climbs, in Britain or on the Continent, are used as scenes for the crimes; and Lewker, as good a mountaineer as he is an actor, brings his technical knowledge to bear in their solution. It might, digressively, be noted that another climber-detective exists: Miss Melinda Pink, a middle-aged JP with incipient arthritis and a weight problem, who earns a comfortable income as a writer for magazines. She appears in novels by Gwen Moffatt (b. 1924), beginning with *Lady with a Cool Eye* (1973).

Nigel Fitzgerald (b. 1906) is the author of a number of well-plotted and extremely readable detective stories set in Ireland, in which full use is made of both the scenery and the local inhabitants. The amateur detective in some of the novels is Alan Russell, an urbane actor-manager, physically a very different type from Lewker—he is described as tall, with a superb physique and a Grecian profile to go with his leonine mane of fair hair (*The Candles Are All Out*, 1960).

Tessa Crichton, a charming young actress, is the heroine-cum-detective-cum-narrator of novels by Anne Morice (pseudonym of Felicity Shaw, b. 1918). In the first, *Death in the Grand Manor* (1970), she meets and falls in love with a handsome police-officer, Robin Price, who becomes her husband; a sensible choice of partner as far as the investigation of crime is concerned. A very similar character is the young Broadway actress Jocelyn O'Roarke, heroine of

Jane Dentinger's *Murder on Cue* (1985), who assists Detective Sergeant Philip Gerrard, described variously as a cross between Tyrone Power and Charles Aznavour or two-thirds Wimsey to one-third Columbo, to solve a murder, falling in love with him in the process. Charles Paris, the detective in *Cast, in Order of Disappearance* (1975) and other novels by Simon Brett (b. 1945), is a rather different type. He is a middle-aged, unsuccessful actor who is separated from his wife and has a drinking problem. The plots are sometimes flimsy; but the books are often very funny, with the author turning a sharply satiric, intolerant eye on the world of the theatre, television, and showbiz generally.

HUSBANDS AND WIVES

This type of detective story is potentially a danger area, offering as it does so much opportunity for sentimentality, whimsy, and baby-talk. The presence of a domestic pet, especially a cat, to whom immoderate attention is paid is a warning sign. Agatha Christie avoids most of these perils in her stories of Tommy and Tuppence Beresford; but the novels, which are usually more thriller than detection, often with an espionage element, are undoubtedly much weaker than the Hercule Poirot or Miss Marple stories. Her couple first appear in *The Secret Adversary* (1922), in which they set the plot in motion by putting an advertisement in a newspaper offering 'two young adventurers for hire'. Dashiell Hammett's *The Thin Man* (1934) has all the ingredients for disaster. Nick and Nora Charles, a retired private detective and his beautiful young wife, are drinking their way through a sociable Christmas in New York, accompanied by Asta, an adorable schnauzer puppy. However, the elliptic, dry, sardonic narrative style—the story is told in the first person by Nick Charles—excludes all sentimentality. Moreover, the book is a brilliant detective story. Hammett wrote no other stories about Mr and Mrs Charles, unfortunately; but the gap was not inadequately filled by the series of films starring William Powell and Myrna Loy which began with *The Thin Man* in 1934. Oddly, though in the book and the first film the thin man of the title is the murder victim, in succeeding films (*After the Thin Man, Another Thin Man*) he is the detective.

The novels by Richard (1898–1982) and Frances (1896–1963) Lockridge about Pamela and Gerald North and their various cats, set in New York City or Florida—*The Norths Meet Murder* (1940) is the first—are less to be recommended. Mrs North's blend of childish scattiness and feminine intuition is less amusing than the authors intend, and the cats are always liable to intrude intolerably into the action. Frances Crane's (b. 1896) couple, Pat and Jean Abbott—in *The Turquoise Shop* (1941)—are less irritating, but also less individual. Though the Abbotts live in San Francisco, they invariably seem to run into trouble on vacation, when local colour can be used to add interest to the intrigue. The stories are narrated by Jean, while the strong, silent Pat does most of the detection. A similar division of labour occurs in Delano Ames's (b. 1906) much more successful and amusing stories about Jane and Dagobert Brown, a very engaging English couple. They have a pleasantly carefree attitude towards life and a capacity for liquor almost equal to that of Nick and Nora Charles (*She Shall Have Murder*, 1949).

Finally, though Chief Inspector—later Detective Chief Superintendent—Henry Tibbett, the detective in novels by Patricia Moyes (b. 1923) is a policeman, his inclusion in this section is justified by the fact that all his cases involve the collaboration, to a greater or less extent, of his wife Emmy. They are a pleasant, unostentatious couple without quirks or eccentricities; and the strength of the novels in which they appear lies in their solid, well-built plots, combined with a good sense of place and a distinctive atmosphere (*Dead Men Don't Ski*, 1959).

FINANCE

One of the most interesting and original detectives of the post-war period is John Putnam Thatcher, senior vice-president and director of the trust department at the Sloan Guaranty Trust of Wall Street, the third largest bank in the world. A distinguished, elderly widower, not only a father but also a grandfather, he is the creation of Mary J. Latis and Martha Hennissart, who together write under the name of Emma Lathen. The authors, one of whom is an attorney, the other an economic analyst, obviously have substantial knowledge of the financial world, and one of the strengths of their books lies in the way in which they put this knowledge to use. The plot is always originated by, and hinges on, some piece of financial fraud or chicanery; and to solve the crime, Thatcher must call on not only his deductive faculty, but also his experience and expertise as a banker. The novels are impeccably written, dryly humorous, with solid, carefully fashioned plots.

Gradually, as the series has progressed, the authors have built up a whole gallery of characters connected with the Sloan, ranging from Bradley Withers, its absentee president, to Miss Corsa, Thatcher's super-efficient secretary; and a good deal of the pleasure that each successive book produces is due to the re-acquaintance not with a single central figure, but with a whole small society (*Banking on Death*, 1961).

Arthur Maling's (b. 1923) novels about Brock Potter, partner in Price, Potter, and Petacque, a New York brokerage house, have the Wall Street financial background in common with Emma Lathen, but little else. Potter is much younger than Thatcher, and narrates the story in the first person. He approximates to the private eye model, and the action therefore tends to be much more violent, with the intrigues often connected with organized crime (*Ripoff*, 1976). Much less serious in tone is the series of novels by David Williams (b. 1926) in which Mark Treasure, an English merchant banker, is the hero and detective—*Unholy Writ* (1976) is the first. Though the action is often set in motion by an event in the world of banking, there is usually no financial angle to the plot or the crime. But the books are light and amusing, and Treasure and his actress-wife good company.

MISCELLANEOUS FEMALE AMATEURS

This group is not large; its best-known member, Agatha Christie's Miss Marple, has already been discussed in the section on private detectives. Of the remainder, the earliest example is Hagar Stanley, a gypsy girl who is the heroine of a group of linked stories—*Hagar of the Pawn-Shop: The Gypsy Detective* (1898)—by Fergus Hume (1859–1932), an author best known for his novel *The Mystery of a Hansom Cab* (1886), which was amazingly popular in its day. Hagar, a girl of 20, is described as having a face 'of the true Romany type: Oriental in its contour and hue, with arched eye-brows over large dark eyes, and a thin-lipped mouth, beautifully shaped, under a delicately-curved nose'. After the death of her uncle, Hagar takes over his pawnshop in Lambeth, in south London, and solves a series of mysteries brought to her by her customers. In fact, though she puzzles out a couple of ciphers, her detection consists of little more than common sense, and she only succeeds where others fail because the latter have been forced by the author wilfully to misunderstand or misinterpret the situation. But the stories, if often melodramatic, are not without ingenuity, and

Hagar, who falls in love in the first and marries in the last, has charm and strength of character.

Equally charming, though in a very different way, is Kyra Sokratesco, a young Rumanian girl who lives on the French Riviera. She is the heroine and detective in two short stories by Gilbert Frankau (1884–1952), 'Who Killed Castelvetro?' (in *Concerning Peter Jackson and Others*, 1931), a story which is frequently anthologized, and 'Tragedy at St Tropez' (in *Experiments in Crime*, 1937). The character and settings are interesting and original; and it is to be regretted that the author, whose other crime stories are considerably less successful, wrote nothing more about Sokratesco. F. Tennyson Jesse's (1889–1958) Solange Fontaine, who appears in *The Solange Stories* (1931), is a similar character. She is half English, half French, has olive-grey eyes, and is 'as straight and as well-knit as an athletic boy'. She is married to a French scientist and assists her father in his work at a police laboratory near Paris. In a foreword to the collection, which treats of the difficulty of writing detective stories, the author explains her choice of a female detective: 'I made the detective a woman because, although I intensely dislike the modern newspaper mode of thought which considers a woman "news", I pandered to it so as to be able to sell my stories more easily.' She adds that the 'theme' of the stories is that 'this woman had been gifted by nature with an extra spiritual sense that warned her of evil'. But the introduction of this supernatural element—in each story Solange has a vision, a precognition of what is to occur—ruins them as detective stories.

Stuart Palmer (1905–68) has said that he based his detective, the lean, horse-faced New York schoolteacher Hildegarde Withers, a spinster in her forties, on two people: his high-school teacher, Miss Fern Hackett, and his father. From them she perhaps takes her incorrigible inquisitiveness—she listens to the police radio and hangs around the headquarters on Center Street—and her impatience with stupidity, her inclination to take over a task that is being done badly. On her first appearance, in *The Penguin Pool Murder* (1931), she acquires a collaborator and admirer, Inspector Oscar Piper of the New York Police Department, a tall, gaunt, melancholy man in a loose topcoat. Both Miss Withers and the inspector are little more than caricatures, and the treatment is at times uncomfortably broad. But the puzzles are well constructed, and the writing is often amusing. In the 1930s six films were made from the books, with Edna May Oliver as a convincing Miss Withers and James Gleason as Oscar Piper.

This relationship between a female detective and a policeman is echoed in Hildegarde Dolson's (1908–81) novels, set in the small Connecticut town of Wingate, which have the pretty, widowed artist Lucy Ramsdale as the detective. Her collaborator is Inspector James MacDougal, who has resigned from the state police homicide division after a humiliating divorce. Though the books avoid the element of caricature, they and the heroine are rather too self-consciously charming, and detection is often overshadowed by domestic detail (*To Spite Her Face*, 1971).

MISCELLANEOUS MALE AMATEURS

Although the detective in most of Dorothy Sayers's work is Lord Peter Wimsey, she also wrote nearly a dozen short stories in which Wimsey is replaced by Montague Egg, a travelling representative from Plummet and Rose, Wines and Spirits, Piccadilly. These appear, mingled with Wimsey stories, in the collections *Hangman's Holiday* (1933) and *In the Teeth of the Evidence* (1939). The stories are neatly and deftly put together, and the detection is genuine enough; but, as Egg's surname suggests, the author is aiming at a broader kind of humour than that which she allows herself when writing of Wimsey. The effect is achieved chiefly by the judicious quotation of rhymed maxims—'The goodwill of the maid is nine-tenths of the trade' and 'If you're a salesman worth the name at all, you can sell razors to a billiard-ball', for example—from the *Salesman's Handbook*, a presumably fictitious compilation which Egg knows by heart. Also in the wine trade, but at a higher level, is Casson Duker, the wine-merchant amateur detective who is the hero of several well-written, original, and interesting novels by William Mole (pseudonym of William Anthony Younger, 1917–62), of which the first is *The Hammersmith Maggot* (1955), in which Duker tracks down an elusive blackmailer.

John Dickson Carr (1906–77) was a prolific author of detective stories, both under his own name and under the pseudonym Carter Dickson. He began with several novels in which the detective is the flamboyant Parisian *juge d'instruction* Henri Bencolin, dealt with below in the chapter on police detectives. In *Hag's Nook* (1933), however, he introduced Dr Gideon Fell, a character modelled on G. K. Chesterton. Fell, a lexicographer, is immensely stout, with a mane of dark hair streaked with white. He loves beer, food, and tobacco; has a vast store of recondite, usually useless information; and is compiling a monumental work entitled *The Drinking Customs of England from the Earliest Days*. In *The Man Who Could Not Shudder* (1940) Carr gives this description of him:

Vast and beaming, wearing a box-pleated cape as big as a tent, he sat . . . with his hands folded over his crutch stick. His shovel hat almost touched the canopy overhead. His eyeglasses were set precariously on a pink nose; the black ribbon of these glasses blew wide with each vast puff of breath which rumbled up from under his three chins and agitated his bandit's moustache. But what you noticed most was the twinkle in his eye. A huge joy of life, a piratical swagger merely to be hearing and seeing and thinking, glowed from him like steam from a furnace. It was like meeting Old King Cole or Father Christmas.

A little later, as Carter Dickson, Carr produced in *The Plague Court Murders* (1934) another eccentric detective, Sir Henry Merrivale, known usually as the Old Man or H. M. Merrivale is bald, pigeon-toed, and barrel-chested. He smokes cigars, scowls evilly, shouts loud and vulgar obscenities when annoyed, and holds one of the oldest baronetcies in England. Though he is head of Intelligence, formerly counter-espionage, at the War Office, he is never seen acting in a professional capacity, but always as an amateur detective. He is more broadly drawn than Fell, and the books in which he appears often contain scenes of pure farce. In *Night at the Mocking Widow* (1950) his suitcase-on-wheels runs away from him, and is pursued down the village street by a pack of dogs. In *Death in Five Boxes* (1938) he is pushing a fruit barrow up a hill when a police car collides with it:

In one majestic crash the barrow whirled, rose and pirouetted like a dancer; at the same time that it exploded with oranges, apples, lemons, Brazil nuts, greengages, and bananas. They did not merely issue from the barrow: they sprayed. The man who had been pushing the barrow escaped its weight; but they saw him turn a kind of Catherine-wheel into the ditch under an avalanche of oranges, apples, lemons, Brazil nuts, greengages, and bananas.

Apart from the names of the detectives, Carr's Fell and Merrivale stories are remarkably similar: they all belong to the puzzle school of detective fiction, exemplified earlier by S. S. Van Dine and Ellery Queen. Carr is undoubtedly the most ingenious of the three—indeed, he is probably the most ingenious of all detective story writers in the creation of puzzles, of crimes committed in impossible situations. His speciality was just this: the seemingly impossible crime, and in particular the locked-room variant of the category. He compiled a longer

list of solutions to this problem than anyone else, and even included
an analytical treatment of the subject—the 'Locked Room Lecture'—
in a Fell novel, *The Hollow Man* (1935; US title *The Three Coffins*).
Though he must be compared to Van Dine and Queen in his approach
to the detective story, his novels have far more life and energy than
theirs. His detectives, if overly eccentric and occasionally irritating,
are never as annoying or as infuriatingly superior as theirs. In addition, the settings, though often fantastic, are never as preposterously
artificial as some of Ellery Queen's. And the novels are often lightened
by the inclusion of a romantic sub-plot involving a young hero—
usually American—and heroine.

   Making the detective a larger-than-life figure, giving him or her a
set of colourful idiosyncrasies, an unusual profession or hobby, all
this had of course the same dual function with the amateur detective
as with the professional. On the one hand, it individualized him and
differentiated him from his rivals; on the other, it circumvented any
difficulties in characterization by substituting eccentricity for personality. No other author went as far in this direction as Carr, but the
majority endeavoured to make their detectives memorable by
employing one or other of these devices. Cyril Hare, whose *An English Murder* has already been discussed, was a notable exception. His
amateur detective, the barrister Francis Pettigrew, who first appears
in *Tragedy at Law* (1942), probably the finest of all detective stories
with a legal background, has neither eccentricities nor idiosyncracies.
Having entered the legal profession with a brilliant academic record,
he had every hope of a spectacularly successful career, but bad luck, a
series of personal difficulties, and, perhaps, a lack of inner conviction
combined to disappoint his expectations. When we first meet him, he
is ageing, unsuccessful, and frustrated, 'eking out a precarious practice by the drudgery of legal authorship'. Later Hare, perhaps mistakenly, relents towards him; and in *With a Bare Bodkin* (1946) he
meets and marries Eleanor Brown, a pretty young woman half his age
with financial expectations. Pettigrew often shares the detective role
with Hare's policeman, Mallett, a character discussed in more detail
in the following chapter; but he also appears alone in several books.
Though Pettigrew is without doubt an amateur detective—he is not
professionally involved in any of the cases with which he deals—most
of Hare's books do have a legal background, and he often uses points
of law to exceedingly good effect in the construction of his plots. Well
written, civilized, and witty, Hare's books must be ranked high

among classical detective stories. And Pettigrew is a flesh-and-blood figure, whose character is affectionately and fully delineated by the author, unlike those detectives who must rely on one or two obvious characteristics or eccentricities for their one-dimensional fictional existence.

Two more legal figures are the fat, cigar-smoking Sir Bruton Kames, Director of Public Prosecutions, and his senior legal assistant, Harvey Tuke, who, with his 'dark and devilish face', resembles Mephistopheles. He has a French wife, and studies the campaigns of Napoleon in his leisure time. Kames and Tuke appear together on a number of cases in novels by Douglas Browne (b. 1884)—*Death Wears a Mask* (1940) is the first. Like Pettigrew, they work as amateurs rather than professionals, although they are obviously able to summon assistance with more authority than most private detectives. And their official position at least ensures that the deferential attitude assumed by the policeman in dealing with the amateur has some justification.

Phoebe Atwood Taylor's (1909–76) Asey Mayo of Wellfleet, on Cape Cod, first encountered in *The Cape Cod Mystery* (1931), is, in Nicholas Blake's words, an 'eccentric original', called variously the Codfish Sherlock or the Homespun Sleuth. A tall, lanky, tobacco-chewing man who habitually wears a canvas jacket, corduroy trousers, and a wide-brimmed stetson, he is a former sailor, speaks with a pronounced Cape Cod accent, and uses his knowledge of human nature and common sense to unravel mysteries that baffle the local police. The author also wrote a number of novels set in Boston under the pseudonym Alice Tilton, in which the detective is Leonidas Witherall, a retired professor, later owner of a boys' prep school. Witherall, called William or Bill because of his remarkable resemblance to portraits of Shakespeare, writes blood-and-thunder thrillers, and is constantly involved in events which imitate his own fiction. The books have little detection in them, and the plot usually turns into a hectic scramble. Indeed, for the way in which they combine crime and farce, they should perhaps be more properly dealt with in the section on comic detectives (*Beginning with a Bash*, 1937).

Morrison Sharpe, the detective in novels by Leslie Cargill, is a chess and puzzle expert, whose skills, when applied to the solution of crimes, enable him to keep a step or two ahead of the police. The novels usually begin well, but tend to degenerate into implausibility (*Death Goes by Bus*, 1936). Clayton Rawson (1906–71) takes the idea further by making his detective, the Great Merlini, a magician. Merlini is not only an accomplished showman; he has also studied magic deeply, written three books on the subject—*Legerdemaniacs*, *The Psychology of Deception*, and *Sawdust Trails*—and owns a shop which supplies magicians and conjurors with the paraphernalia of their trade. He brings his knowledge to bear on a series of seemingly impossible locked-room mysteries (*Death from a Top Hat*, 1938). Two other detectives with a show-business background—that of a carnival—are Ed Hunter and his uncle Ambrose, who appear in novels by Fredric Brown (1906–72). In the first, *The Fabulous Clip-joint* (1947), Ambrose leaves his job with a carnival to help Ed track down his father's murderer. Later the pair set up a small private detective agency in Chicago.

The novels by Tod Claymore (pseudonym of Hugh Clevely) use the Ellery Queen method: the detective is also the author, though the stories are told in the first person rather than the third. Claymore starts out as a tennis professional, is in the RAF during the war, and later comes to Florida. There is little detection in the novels, and the plots are uncoordinated; the interest lies in the recurrent difficulties and hairbreadth escapes that befall the narrator, while in the later books, set in America, his relationship with his pre-adolescent daughter Sarah is entertaining and well portrayed (*You Remember the Case*, 1939; US title *This Is What Happened*).

Elizabeth Daly's (1878–1967) Henry Gamadge (in *Unexpected Night*, 1940), though American, has many of the characteristics of the English amateur detective. Indeed, Anthony Boucher has written of him that he is 'a man so well-bred as to make Lord Peter Wimsey seem a trifle coarse'. Physically, however, he bears no resemblance to the earlier handsome man-about-town type. Though tall, he has blunt features, grey-green eyes, and mouse-coloured hair; his expensive, well-cut suits always look ill-fitting and ill-pressed. He is an author and bibliophile, whose knowledge of manuscripts, *incunabula*, and first editions often proves useful in solving cases. He lives in the exclusive Murray Hill district of New York, together with Theodore, a black servant; Harold Bantz, his assistant; and Martin, a cat. In later novels he acquires a pretty young wife, Clara, and a son. A pseudo-supernatural element in some of the novels is distinctly irritating; and Elizabeth Daly, like a number of other authors, is given to assigning domestic detail and cats an overly large role in the narrative. But the stories are usually genuine examples of detection, while Gamadge himself is an efficient reasoner who, though a distinct individual, is far from being excessively eccentric.

The three detective stories by Edgar Box—*Death in the Fifth Position* (1952) is the first—are notable chiefly because the author's name conceals the identity of Gore Vidal (b. 1925), better known as a straight novelist. In all three the detective-narrator is Peter Cutler Sargeant II, a smart, suave young Ivy Leaguer who runs a small public relations agency. Detection is limited, and the plots are carelessly tied together, but the style is elegant and witty. Sex, hitherto the preserve of the private eye, plays a large part in Sargeant's life, but is treated neither pruriently nor pornographically.

Judson Philips, whose one-legged columnist Peter Styles was discussed in the previous chapter, has also, under the pseudonym Hugh Pentecost, written a number of novels, beginning with *The Cannibal who Overate* (1962), in which the amateur detective is Pierre Chambrun, resident manager of the Hotel Beaumont, described by the author as the 'top luxury residence hotel in New York'. Chambrun was born in France, but came to America as a boy. He is a short, dark, stocky man, with heavy pouches under his dark eyes. His energies and his detective ability, honed by his experiences as a member of the French resistance during the Second World War, are devoted to the smooth, efficient running of the hotel. The hotel, of course, is a perfect setting for romance, mystery, and intrigue as Arnold Bennett with *The Grand Babylon Hotel* (1902) and Vicki Baum with *Grand Hotel* (1931; originally *Menschen im Hotel*, 1929) had shown earlier, and the Chambrun stories, probably the most effective of this author's manifold production, make a cruder, but still effective, use of the background.

Michael Delving (pseudonym of Jay Williams, 1914–78) uses as detectives, either separately or together, two American antique dealers and rare booksellers: Dave Cannon, a Connecticut Yankee, and Bob Eddison, a Cherokee Indian—*Smiling, the Boy Fell Dead* (1967) is the first. The first novels in the series are set in Britain, in Wales or Gloucestershire, where both heroes find wives. The intrigue often revolves around an antique: a rare book, for example, a manuscript, or, on one occasion, a gold-rimmed wooden bowl said to be the Holy Grail. Two other writers, Jonathan Gash (pseudonym of John Grant, b. 1933) and John Malcolm, use a similar background. Gash's hero, Lovejoy, is a lecherous, penurious East Anglian antique dealer, as often on the wrong side of the law as the right, and as skilled at faking antiques as recognizing them. Amusing as the books are, the narration is often overburdened with irrelevant, if fascinating, information on antiques; and as a result, plots can become haphazard and less than convincing (*The Judas Pair*, 1977). Tim Simpson, the hero-narrator of John Malcolm's series of novels, an amateur art expert and ex-rugby player, works initially for a firm of investment consultants, but is then recruited by a merchant bank to run its art investment fund. Again, a justifiable criticism might be that the information on, for example, Sickert's life and work in *A Back Room in Somers Town* (1984), the first of the series, is excessive and redundant; but it is interesting all the same, and perhaps more successfully integrated into the plot than the information on antiques is in Gash's books. This criticism does not recognize, however, that Gash and Malcolm have both departed from the usual form of the detective story in that the object at the centre of each novel, the painting or antique, together with its provenance and creator, are in the end more important than the mystery, the deductions, and the solution.

Chapter 4

THE POLICE

'Have you any idea of the disadvantages under which a detective labours? For instance now, you imagine that I can insinuate myself into all sorts of society perhaps, but are mistaken. Strange as it may appear, I have never by any possibility of means succeeded with one class of persons at all, I cannot pass myself off for a gentleman.'

(Anna K. Green, *The Leavenworth Case*)

Despite the example given by Gaboriau with Lecoq, the police detective novel was far slower getting off the ground than either the amateur detective or the private detective story. The reason for the policeman's lack of popularity seems to have been twofold. On the one hand, the image of the police detective canonized by Conan Doyle and imitated by other writers in the figures of Lestrade, Athelney Jones, and Holmes's other official rivals was that of a plodding, unimaginative investigator, whose deductions and conclusions were invariably not merely wrong, but laughably wrong. Such a figure could hardly be placed at the centre of a narrative or allowed to solve the most intricate of crimes. In addition, there was the problem intimated in the words of Ebenezer Gryce, Anna K. Green's (1846–1935) police detective, placed at the head of this chapter: that of the policeman's social position. While the police were quite capable of dealing with the brutal, common and sordid crimes committed among the general populace, they were not only intellectually, but also socially, incapable of comprehending the nuances of the more subtle, refined, delicately plotted murders met with among the upper classes. More than this, while they might feel at ease in the servants' hall and be able to carry out an efficient interrogation of a kitchen-maid or a cook, when confronted with a landowner, nobleman, or tycoon, they found themselves out of their social depth; though they might represent the full majesty of the law, they could be browbeaten, insulted, and even ignored. Gaboriau makes use of this contrast in his *M. Lecoq*. As long as the suspect whom Lecoq pursues through the streets and lodging-houses of Paris is thought to be an indigent circus showman named May, the policeman's actions are free and unconstrained. But once May is tentatively identified as the Duc de Sairmeuse, Lecoq becomes helpless. It is presumably for this reason that, when reading police detective novels of the 1920s and 1930s, one is occasionally conscious of a slight feeling of unease on the part of the author—rather akin to the feeling of unease experienced by the heroine's relatives in E. M. Forster's *Where Angels Fear to Tread* on learning that she is to marry a dentist: both having as their cause the anomalous social position of the character, dentist or policeman, who is certainly not a servant, but equally certainly not a gentleman. Authors have developed various strategems to deal with this unease.

Anna K. Green's Ebenezer Gryce, who first appears in *The Leavenworth Case: A Lawyer's Story* (1878), is a throw-back to the earlier detectives of the century: to Collins's Sergeant Cuff and Dickens's Inspector Bucket. There is an apparent attempt at the Dickensian manner, for example, in the way in which the narrator, Everett Raymond, a gentlemanly lawyer who falls in love with one of two beautiful sisters, both suspects, describes Gryce at their first meeting:

Mr Gryce was a portly, comfortable personage with an eye that never pounced, that did not even rest—on you. If it rested anywhere, it was always on some insignificant object in your vicinity, some vase, inkstand, book or button. These things he would seem to take into his confidence, make the repositories of his conclusions, but you—you might as well be the steeple on Trinity Church, for all the connection you ever appeared to have with him or his thoughts.

The plot, however, a well-put-together Victorian melodrama, owes more to the methods of Collins in works such as *The Woman in White* than it does to Dickens. As detective novels the books seem heavy-going now, and are perhaps most interesting as representations of the manners of society in New York and Washington in the final quarter of the last century.

A. E. W. Mason (1865–1948), a successful playwright and a novelist in several genres, produced his first detective story, *At the Villa Rose*, in 1910. It is set in Aix-les-Bains, and in it Mason introduced Inspector Hanaud, an agent of the French Sûreté. Stout and broad-shouldered, with a full, heavy face, he looks like a prosperous comedian. Occasionally there can be something 'elephantinely selfish' about his behaviour; and he is described by another character as 'a heavy, clever, middle-aged man, liable to become a little gutterboy at a moment's notice'. He calls detectives 'servants of chance', whose skill is 'to seize quickly the hem of her skirt when it flashes for a fraction of a second' before their eyes. Though he is a French policeman, Hanaud owes nothing to Gaboriau. He is, rather, another example of the popular type of the time, the great detective. He is secretive, prone to mystification, and will explain the course his reasoning has taken only after the denouement of the story. He has his Watson in the guise of Mr Ricardo, a retired widower in his early fifties who has made a fortune in Mincing Lane. Though Ricardo is not the narrator, the reader is allowed to know only as much as Ricardo knows. Hanaud, like Holmes, delights in teasing his collaborator with enigmatic remarks, and indulges in some none too subtle sarcasm at Ricardo's expense on the frequent occasions when the latter, trying to exhibit his intelligence, succeeds only in making a fool of himself. Hanaud, like many Frenchmen in English fiction, is a broadly drawn, semi-comic character; but he is less of a caricature, less a collection of eccentric traits, than Agatha Christie's Hercule Poirot, whose conception obviously owes much to Mason's character. But if Hanaud is more subtly portrayed, as a fictional detective he is less satisfactory than Poirot. This stems partly from his refusal to divulge any of his deductions or conclusions to Ricardo during the investigation, thus keeping both Ricardo and the reader from any real participation in the work of detection—this may heighten suspense, but it certainly reduces interest—and partly from the sensational, melodramatic quality of the situations portrayed in the novels.

For the sake of completeness another of Baroness Orczy's creations should be mentioned here, Lady Molly Robertson-Kirk, head of the Female Department of Scotland Yard, whose exploits, narrated by her secretary, form a collection of short stories entitled *Lady Molly of Scotland Yard* (1910). Her most notable achievement is to establish the innocence of her husband, Captain Hubert de Mazareen, who has been convicted for the murder of his grandfather's solicitor and is serving a sentence at Dartmoor prison.

INSPECTOR FRENCH

For the first serious, professional police detective it was necessary to wait until 1920, when Freeman Wills Crofts (1879–1957) made his début with *The Cask*, in which Inspector Burnley investigates the murder of a young Frenchwoman whose body has been discovered at London Docks in a cask supposedly containing statuary. The book is a milestone in the history of the detective novel. Although it retained some of the melodramatic qualities of its predecessors—of which Crofts was gradually to rid himself—at the same time it took over and developed the best qualities of Gaboriau. Crofts's policeman is the antithesis of the great detective; he has no Watson to astound with brilliant deductions, nor does he keep his ratiocinations concealed from the reader. His detection is solid, plodding, and logical, with an almost fanatical devotion to detail. The reader is privy to every step in the slow—at times almost agonizing—construction of a theory of the crime until the final solution is triumphantly reached. Crofts was a Northern Irishman who worked for the Belfast and Northern Counties Railway, rising to the position of chief assistant engineer; but in 1929 he resigned to become a full-time writer. It is not surprising, therefore, not only that some of his books should have a North of Ireland setting, but also that the plots of many of them turn on railway technicalities. Just as John Dickson Carr specialized in the locked-room mystery, so Crofts specializes in the unbreakable alibi, often built up, with virtuosity and imagination, from the railway timetable. His plots are put together with the care and precision of an engineer: indeed, Raymond Chandler has called him 'the soundest builder of them all'. His weaknesses are a certain predictability, in that it is often possible to identify the criminal early on as the suspect with the best alibi; an occasional dullness in narration; and a style which serves as a means of communication, but little else. After *The Cask* Crofts wrote three novels, *The Ponson Case* (1921), *The Pit-Prop Syndicate* (1922), and *The Groote Park Murder* (1924), in each of which the detective is a different policeman. With his next novel, challengingly entitled *Inspector French's Greatest Case* (1925), however, he created his series detective, whom he went on to employ in nearly thirty novels and a number of short stories. Inspector Joseph French is stout, below middle height, with a clean-shaven, good-humoured face and dark blue eyes. Known behind his back at the Yard as 'Soapy Joe' because of the way he relies on the suavity of his manners, he is happily married, and often turns to his wife, Emily, for advice when he reaches a difficult stage in a case. He is fond of good food—his meals are often described in detail—and enjoys travel, whether on holiday or on duty. In fact, he differs from Crofts's earlier detectives only in that he is described more fully and given a home background; as far as method of detection goes, Crofts's policemen are indistinguishable from one another. They are all alike in other respects too: solid, bourgeois *fonctionnaires* who have come up through the ranks of the police force and have no pretensions to be other than they are. Nor is there the slightest hint that Crofts feels ill at ease in their company.

French was followed during the next few years by a number of police detectives who bear, to a greater or less extent, a family resemblance to him. They are all members of the same social class, all of approximately the same rank and age—somewhere in the forties, which allows them an avuncular, at times even fatherly, attitude to young suspects, witnesses, and police constables. We see them all at work, watch them collecting minute pieces of evidence and putting them slowly and painstakingly together to solve a crime. G. D. H. and M. Cole's Superintendent Henry Wilson, who first appears in *The Brooklyn Murders* (1923) by G. D. H. Cole alone, is 'a tall man, with quick nervous movements, and a curious way of closing his eyes and holding up his hands before him with the tips of his fingers pressed tightly together when he was discussing a case', who, like French, will consult his wife, a stout, motherly figure, when he is at a standstill.

Agatha Christie's Superintendent Battle, 'a squarely-built middle-aged man with a face so singularly devoid of expression as to be quite remarkable' (*The Secret of Chimneys*, 1925), is the same type of character, though the situation in which he is involved here is far too sensational and far-fetched for a detective story; in later novels he tends to appear only as a foil to Poirot.

Superintendent Ross, who appears in novels (*The Eye in the Museum*, 1929) by J. J. Connington (pseudonym of Alfred Walter Stewart, 1880–1947), is closer to French in type. However, he is a member of a provincial police force rather than Scotland Yard, and is decidedly quicker on the uptake than French. The author was professor of chemistry at Queen's University, Belfast, from 1914 to 1944, and wrote a well-known series of works on various branches of chemistry; in the telling use he makes of scientific knowledge he resembles R. Austin Freeman. Though Connington is a brighter narrator than Crofts, compared to French Ross is a relatively anonymous figure, being described only as 'a big, clean-shaven man' in a grey suit with a grey felt hat. He gives the impression of a 'kindly, free and easy fellow who'd get on well with most people'; but we learn nothing more about his appearance, character, or domestic situation. Much more successful in this respect is Connington's other series of police detective novels, discussed below, in which the central figure is Chief Constable Sir Clinton Driffield.

W. Stanley Sykes (b. 1894) also emulates Freeman in the use of medical and scientific detail in *The Missing Money-Lender* (1931; US title *The Man Who Was Dead*). Among the author's other works is *A Manual of General Medical Practice* (1927); so it is not too surprising that the murder method should be medically ingenious, or that the novel should end with Inspector Drury of Scotland Yard being shown how to use a polarimeter to detect the difference between glucose and laevulose. Sykes wrote only two novels with Drury as the detective, but both are certainly worth reading. Drury is probably the most physically imposing of all fictional policemen; he is six foot two and a half inches tall, weighs fifteen stone; and before joining the force, played rugby for England and rugby league as a professional.

Most of this group of policemen, like French, are stout; and Superintendent Fillinger, the detective in novels by Paul McGuire (1903–78) is more than that. He is an enormous man, with 'small round piggish eyes', who turns the scales at some twenty-nine stone, which would make him more than six stone heavier than Nero Wolfe. But he carries his weight with more agility, and is often compared to the Italian boxer Primo Carnera (*The Tower Mystery*, 1932; US title *Death Tolls the Bell*).

Inspector Meredith is the detective in a number of solid, workman-like novels by John Bude (pseudonym of Ernest Carpenter Elmore, 1901–57), which usually make good use of real topography—*The Lake District Murder* (1935) is the first.

Cyril Hare's Inspector Mallett has been mentioned in passing in the previous chapter in conjunction with Hare's amateur detective, Pettigrew. The two appear both together and separately; on Mallett's first appearance, in *Tenant for Death* (1938), he is alone. He is a tall, stout man with bright grey eyes 'set in a large red face, the geniality of which was oddly contradicted by a fierce, pointed military moustache'. He has an encyclopaedic knowledge of London's byways and alleys—his 'Forty-two routes from the Old Bailey to Scotland Yard' is, we are told, a minor classic of police literature. He is even fonder of food than French; indeed, he finds his brain refuses to work unless provided with an adequate supply of sustenance: 'How could an all-too-human detective attend to the matters in hand when his thoughts would keep straying to a nicely grilled steak and tomato, with boiled apple pudding and cheese to follow?' In this, of course, his experience runs counter to that of Sherlock Holmes, who found that his brain could only reach a peak of efficiency if his body were starved. Hare is always a pleasure to read, and his plots are ingenious; indeed, the Inspector Mallett stories are among the best in this group.

YOUNGER POLICEMEN

The prototype provided by Freeman Wills Crofts in Inspector French did not suit all authors, of course. For some he was too old; for others he belonged to the wrong social class. In 1923, in *Hounded Down*, David Durham (pseudonym of Roy Vickers, 1888?–1965) produced a rather different figure in the shape of Inspector Rason. 'Of good family and liberal education, he had during the war held the rank of colonel in the Intelligence Department, and at the Yard he was regarded as a future Chief Commissioner.' Vickers confused the issue, however, by creating another Inspector Rason, a police-officer of the French type, in the short stories he wrote under his own name which deal with the Department of Dead Ends, a fictional department of Scotland Yard where evidence of unsolved crimes is kept (*The Department of Dead Ends*, 1949).

Following Vickers, Henry Wade (pseudonym of Sir Henry Lancelot Aubrey Fletcher, 6th baronet, 1887–1969) created Detective Inspector John Poole (*The Duke of York's Steps*, 1929). Poole has been educated at a public school and at the fictional St James's College, Oxford, where he read law and obtained a half-blue for athletics. Wade spends rather too much time, perhaps, explaining why Poole, while at college, should have conceived the odd ambition of joining the police force and rising to become head of the Criminal Investigation Department at Scotland Yard. And the details he gives of Poole's career—that he is called to the Bar, joins the Metropolitan Police at 23, is transferred to the CID after fifteen months, made sergeant at 27, and then, put down for accelerated promotion, becomes a detective inspector—do not completely succeed in convincing us of its probability. Poole is very different from French, not only socially but also physically: nearly six feet in height, he has 'the straight hips, small waist and wide shoulders of the ideal athlete'. His chin is well moulded rather than strong, his mouth quietly firm, and he has grey, steady eyes. In other words, the new policeman is young, handsome, and often well educated. Poole improves and gains character with time, and becomes more convincing in Wade's later novels. But whatever criticisms might be levelled at Poole on his first appearance, there can be no doubt that Wade is one of the outstanding authors not only of the thirties, but also of the immediate post-war period. His novels are varied in plot and situation; they have wit, and his style is forceful and elegant.

A similar character, though realized much less well, is E. R. Punshon's (1872–1956) Bobby Owen, who appears in a large number of mediocre novels, beginning with *Information Received* (1933). Owen, who starts out as a constable, but by 1940 has worked his way up to detective sergeant, is also a handsome, athletic young man with an Oxford education, though he took only a pass degree. He does not have Poole's dedication to a police career, having joined the force only because he preferred it to the Army.

Sir Basil Thomson, who was head of the CID at Scotland Yard during the First World War, wrote a number of novels in which the hero is Richardson, a young Scot from Arbroath, who begins as a constable in *P. C. Richardson's First Case* (1933) and ends as chief constable in *A Murder Arranged* (1937; US title *When Thieves Fall Out*), surely the most remarkable instance of accelerated promotion in the history of the police force. Richardson is another faceless character; he has no individual characteristics whatsoever, not even a first name. The books are plodding and unimaginative, but have some dry humour and a certain amount of charm in their depiction of the London scene. Their description of police procedures is more realistic than that of most other authors, and in this respect they adumbrate the later police-procedural novels discussed below.

In 1931 Lord Trenchard, creator of the RAF, was asked by the Government to become commissioner for the Metropolitan Police, whose morale and efficiency then gave grounds for concern. Among his reforms were the creation of a police college and forensic laboratory at Hendon and a ten-year engagement scheme for police-officers. The result was that in a short space of time the number of university graduates in the police force rose sharply, making a character like Poole much less of an aberration. Inspector George Martin, who first appears in *The Norwich Victims* (1935) by Francis Beeding (pseudonym of John Leslie Palmer, 1885–1944, and Hilary Aidan St George Saunders, 1898–1951), is an example of the new breed of policeman. The original edition of the book is possibly unique among detective stories in that the text is preceded by photographs of all the main characters. From these we can see that Martin is a fine, upstanding young man with a firm jaw who favours a plaid tie. In the novel he is contrasted with a colleague, Crosby, who has worked himself up from a beat at Whitechapel to the rank of inspector. Martin, university-educated, is the son of a doctor at Cromer; Crosby comes from an orphanage. Martin is a Conservative; Crosby is Labour, verging on Communist. Despite these differences, in Beeding's fictional world they are the best of friends and work well together. The book is free of the facetiousness which tends to mar Beeding's spy stories, and has a genuinely surprising denouement.

Margaret Erskine's (pseudonym of Margaret Wetherby Williams, d. 1984) detective, Inspector Septimus Finch, is very similar in type to Wade's Inspector Poole. Son of a well-known West Country lawyer, Finch entered the police force as a constable from public school, and has been rapidly promoted. Physically he resembles Poole, having 'the narrow hips and wide shoulders of an athlete' and a 'pleasant, nondescript face' (*And Being Dead*, 1938; US title *The Limping Man*; also in US as *The Painted Mask*).

Michael Gilbert's (b. 1912) *Close Quarters*, though published in 1947, was written before the war, and thus belongs to this period. One of the detectives, Sergeant Bobby Pollock, as nephew of the dean of Melchester and as an ex-public schoolboy, obviously belongs to this group of younger policemen; his superior, however, Chief Inspector Hazlerigg, 'a thick square man with a brick-red face', who was to become Gilbert's regular police detective, is much more in the French mould, resembling most closely, perhaps, Connington's Superintendent Ross. The novel is one of the best of its kind, wittily written and extremely well put together. The canons of Melchester Cathedral provide a gallery of interestingly eccentric divines.

A number of other detectives who fit the pattern of the youngish, handsome, well-educated policeman might be mentioned quickly here, beginning with George Goodchild's (b. 1888) handsome and masterful Inspector McLean, hero of a long series of novels, beginning with *McLean of Scotland Yard* (1929) and E. C. R. Lorac's (pseudonym of Edith Caroline Rivett, 1894–1958) Detective Inspector Macdonald, 'lean and wiry, dark-headed and dark-eyed'

(*The Murder on the Burrows*, 1931). An odd feature of this book is that
Inspector Macdonald appears to be superior in rank to Superintendent
Jenkins, who takes Macdonald's orders and imitates his methods,
speech, and even his clothes. Under the alternative pseudonym of
Carol Carnac the same author produced Inspector Ryvet of Scotland
Yard, who has a 'cleancut face, slightly aquiline in feature, smooth
fair hair and reflective grey-blue eyes' (*Triple Death*, 1936)—in other
words, a replica of Lord Peter Wimsey. Again as Carnac, she later
wrote of an older version of this character, Chief Inspector Julian
Rivers, 'a big fair fellow, neat and well-built' (*A Double for Detection*,
1945). As a lean contrast to his earlier Superintendent Fillinger, Paul
McGuire presents Detective Inspector Cummings of Scotland Yard,
as fastidious in his attire as Wimsey, who is always addressed as Mr
Cummings (*Murder in Bostall*, 1931).

MORE CULTURED POLICEMEN

Other writers, while accepting the fundamental characteristics of the
Inspector French model—age, avuncularity, and, to a large extent,
social class—obviously found the original a tedious companion, with
few interests other than work and a deplorable lack of culture. They
proceeded to remedy the situation by producing a series of middle-
aged, hard-working policemen who are yet capable of displaying
knowledge in diverse fields almost in the manner of the amateur
detective. Victor MacClure's (b. 1887) Chief Dectective Inspector
Archie Burford, for example, the detective in a series of novels of varied
quality, some of which are still readable, astonishes his Oxford-
educated sergeant with apposite quotations from Shakespeare.
Burford has one physical characteristic which is probably unique
among fictional detectives: when on the scent of a clue, his ears flatten
back against his head, giving him the appearance of a flayed cat (*The
Counterfeit Murders*, 1932).

Inspector Cheviot Burmann, the detective in some thirty novels by
Belton Cobb (1892–1971)—*No Alibi* (1936) is the first—is differen-
tiated from the common herd of policemen by his uncommon name.
Apart from this, he is a colourless character, as is Cobb's other
policeman, Superintendent Manning (*Early Morning Poison*, 1947).
But socially, both are a cut or two above French.

Much more sharply defined and individual is Inspector Charlton of
the Downshire County Constabulary CID, who appears in novels by

Clifford Witting (b. 1907). A big man, who habitually wears a dark grey overcoat and a bowler hat, he is broad-shouldered, with thick, greying hair. In *Murder in Blue* (1937), the first of the series, John Rutherford, proprietor of a small bookshop pretentiously named *Voslivres*, who marries Charlton's niece Molly at the end of the novel, describes the impression the inspector makes on him at their first meeting: 'His deep voice was gentle and cultured, and his lips seemed always ready to smile. He rather reminded me of one of those prosperous doctors, whose large practices make demands not so much upon their professional ability, as upon their social qualities. He had—how shall I say it?—a *comforting* air.' In fact, as Rutherford later learns, Charlton's nickname among his colleagues is 'the Doctor'; and his soothing bedside manner lures those he is questioning into revealing more than they mean to. The best of the books are exceedingly agreeable to read, and Charlton is always civilized and charming. In later novels the detective is Peter Bradfield, who begins as a detective constable and then becomes Charlton's sergeant.

Charlton is undoubtedly avuncular; so, too, is Chief Inspector Dan Pardoe, described as a 'Universal Uncle' in Dorothy Bowers's *Postscript to Poison* (1938). He is a tall man nearing 40, with 'a finely shaped head, the lean, red, sensitive face of an out-of-doors man, and strong curly hair that was already almost white'. Superintendent Mallett, in novels by Mary Fitt (pseudonym of Kathleen Freeman, 1897–1959), is, like so many detectives, a Scot; he is also physically not unlike his namesake, Cyril Hare's Inspector Mallett, being 'tall, massively built, weatherbeaten in the face, with green shrewd eyes, a ginger moustache and a Scots accent' (*Sky Rocket*, 1938). Another Scot is G. V. Galwey's (b. 1912) detective, Chief Inspector 'Daddy' Bourne, more paternal than avuncular. He appears in three novels, of which *Murder on Leave* (1946) is the first. If his nickname indicates his closeness to the Inspector French prototype, he is at the same time differentiated from it by his other characteristics: he reads Trollope in his spare time, and has an intriguing relationship, pursued throughout the novels, with two women, a mother—whom he marries in the last book—and her journalist-daughter.

PERIPHERAL POLICEMEN

The police detective novel may begin immediately with a crime—the discovery of a body, for instance. Or this may be postponed, and the opening chapters used to construct a social setting and indicate the presence within it of suppressed passions and latent hostilities. The crime is then committed, the police are brought in, and the rest of the novel is an account of their investigation. When the second method is adopted, with the entry of the police an abrupt change in the narrative point of view takes place: the author moves from a broad, quasi-omniscient point of view to something much narrower, circumscribed by the investigator's knowledge. Some authors, irked by this restriction, prefer to keep their attention on the society of the novel as a whole, rather than concentrate on the detective in particular. The method has another advantage, in that it keeps the intrusions of the police to a minimum; the inspector is relegated to the status of a peripheral figure, social embarrassments are overcome, and much of the investigation—or at least speculation and deduction—is carried out by the rest of the cast. The supreme practitioner of this method is Georgette Heyer (1902–74), who employs it in a series of amusing, charmingly written, well-plotted novels which have as the detective first Superintendent Hannasyde (*Death in the Stocks*, 1935; US title *Merely Murder*) and later Inspector Hemingway, who begins as Hannasyde's sergeant (*No Wind of Blame*, 1939). In each she constructs a small closed society of characters, usually resident in a large country house or small village in the Home Counties, provides a universally disliked victim, and then follows the course not only of the murder investigation, but also of several entwined love-affairs, before simultaneously bringing detection and courtships to a happy ending. Her detective stories are similar to her Regency romances in many ways. Both exhibit a complex plot, usually with a heroine who is either a scatter-brained blonde or a level-headed brunette, and a dark, sardonic, forceful hero. The books certainly deserve to be ranked with those of Sayers, Allingham, and Marsh; if she does not attain the heights of the first, she has a surer, less erring touch than the latter two.

Christianna Brand (1909–88) often uses a similar method in her stories with Inspector Cockrill of the Kent County Police as the investigator. But Cockrill usually plays a larger part than Hannasyde or Hemingway. As a local man, not a detective summoned from Scotland Yard, he often knows the situation and the characters already. Further, he is made more distinctive through careful description: a little man, he looks older than he is, has bright brown eyes, an aquiline nose, and fingers stained dark brown from the constant rolling of cigarettes, and dresses in a shabby raincoat with a hat crammed carelessly down on his head (*Heads You Lose*, 1941).

To this group can be added, finally, Peter Dickinson's (b. 1927) novels about the ageing, grey, unglamorous Superintendent Jimmy Pibble of Scotland Yard. These are slightly different from the novels of the two previous authors in that the policeman and his investigation are not peripheral to the society which forms the centre of the novel, but are integrated into it. However, the society itself, different in each book, is so strange and outré, so complex in its detail, and demands so much narrative attention that the detection is necessarily subordinated to it. In *Skin Deep* (1968; US title *The Glass-Sided Ants' Nest*), for example, the first of the series, Pibble investigates the murder of the chief of a New Guinea tribe which has been installed in a Victorian house in London by a rich, scholarly anthropologist, daughter of the missionary who converted the tribe to Christianity. The novels are over-rich in their setting, perhaps, but their ingenuity and the quality of the writing cannot be denied.

THE AMATEUR PROFESSIONAL

The simplest way to create a socially acceptable policeman, one in whose company the author feels wholly at ease, is to turn the amateur detective of the young man-about-town variety into an official one. This is a road down which a large number of authors travelled in the 1920s and 1930s: the literature of this period is full of young, handsome, usually bachelor—though they meet and may marry suspects in the course of their careers—police inspectors. Like their amateur counterparts, they have stores of esoteric and miscellaneous knowledge, cram their conversation with literary allusions, often of an arcane kind, are distressingly inclined to babble in facetious—and only occasionally amusing—fashion, are frequently accompanied by civilian Watsons whom they mystify with enigmatic remarks, dress well, have an air of distinction, and unmistakably belong to the right social class—so much so that the novels ring with a constant refrain of astonishment as characters come to realize that the impeccably suited gentleman who has just handed them his card is, unbelievably, a copper. The type is as implausible as its model, the amateur detective, of course. But whereas it is the situation of the amateur detective which fails to convince, with the amateur policeman it is the implausibility of his character.

A. Fielding (pseudonym of Dorothy Feilding, b. 1884) wrote a number of slow-moving, and on the whole tedious, novels in which the detective is Chief Inspector Pointer, a 'tall, slender, bronzed-faced, youngish man' (*The Eames-Erskine Case*, 1924). He lives in Bayswater, liking its 'open spaces and cleaner air'; and the description of the flat he shares with a friend almost rivals that of Philo Vance's apartment, aesthetically speaking. The huge drawing-room has 'ivory walls and paint . . . thick, short draw-curtains of apple-green silk . . . chair covers of a Persian pattern—green leaves rioting over a cream ground, with here and there a pomegranate or a white bird'. The description of food is also reminiscent of Vance: Pointer's land-lady serves up vegetable soup, potato salad, and 'Tartar *bitokes*—savoury balls of beefsteak and marrow and seasonings pounded to perfection and browned to a turn'. Pointer does not exhibit many of the characteristics of the type, however, and becomes more colourless as the series progresses.

Inspector Alan Grant, the detective in novels by Josephine Tey (pseudonym of Elizabeth MacKintosh, 1897–1952; also the author of plays and novels under the name of Gordon Daviot), is a more typical example. He is introduced in *The Man in the Queue* (1929, originally as by Gordon Daviot; US title *Killer in the Crowd*). Grant is a bache-lor and lives in lodgings, where he is ministered to by an admiring landlady. He is of medium height, slight, and 'sartorially chic', and has, he is told by an artist, 'a charming head'. He has inherited a considerable legacy, which enables him to dine at restaurants as fashionable as Laurent's, where he is one of the five people in Europe who are pets of Marcel, the head waiter. Moreover, he is certainly never taken for what he is; when Miss Lethbridge comes into her drawing-room expecting to find an ordinary policeman, 'The sight of the police officer in reality was so astonishing that she looked again at his card quite involuntarily, and Grant smiled inwardly a little more broadly than he permitted himself outwardly.' *The Man in the Queue*, though highly readable, is disappointing as detection; Josephine Tey's later works improve considerably on this, however. The settings are interesting; and Grant emerges as a distinct character and as one of the more sympathetic examples of this type of detective. It is a relief, too, that the author keeps him from facetiousness.

Unfortunately this is not true of the character who is probably the best-known detective of this group: Chief Inspector—later Superin-tendent—Roderick Alleyn, hero of a long series of books by Ngaio Marsh (1899–1982), beginning with *A Man Lay Dead* (1934), in which his rank is eccentrically given as chief inspector detective. Educated at Oxford, Alleyn entered the diplomatic service, but resigned in order to go into the police. Tall, dark, and thin, he has been dubbed 'Handsome Alleyn' by the Press; female characters tend to compare his head to that of a monk or a Spanish grandee. Little detail is given of his family, but, with a mother called Lady Alleyn who breeds Alsatians, there can be little doubt that he belongs to the aristocracy. He begins as a bachelor, but in the course of one of his investigations meets the painter Agatha Troy, and marries her a book later. Again, he is far from resembling a policeman. In *Surfeit of Lampreys* (1940; US title *Death of a Peer*) a young New Zealand girl, Roberta Grey, looking back at the murder, remembers that

until Alleyn appeared, an image of a fictitious detective had hung about at the back of all her thoughts; an image of a man coldly attentive with coarse hands and a large soapy-shining face. Alleyn was so little like this image that for a moment she thought he must be some visitor, fantastically *de trop*, who had dropped in to see the Lampreys. The sight of Fox disabused her of this idea. There was no mistake about Fox.

Inspector Fox, facetiously called 'Br'er Fox' or 'Foxkin' by Alleyn, is a hero-worshipping subordinate, who alternates between treating Alleyn as a friendly divinity and a fractious child. At the beginning Alleyn has a Watson in the form of a young journalist, Nigel Bathgate, but the author sensibly abandons him in later books. Ngaio Marsh plots well, creates convincing characters, and places them in interesting and varied settings. She sets several novels in her native New Zealand, and is particularly fond of employing a theatrical background, reflecting her work for the stage. Like Georgette Heyer, she will often devote as much attention to the characters and society of the novel as to the detection, though Alleyn never becomes as peripheral a figure as Hemingway or Hannasyde. Like Heyer again, the intrigue is often filled out with one or more romantic sub-plots. On the other hand, detail, especially of a technical kind, is often carelessly done, and the snobbery is no less overt than that of Dorothy Sayers.

However implausible these characters may seem, they are certainly intended to perform the function of, and bear some resemblance to, real policemen. This is not the case, however, with the characters in the novels of Michael Innes (pseudonym of John Innes Mackintosh Stewart, b. 1906). Innes's detective is John Appleby, who rises from inspector to commissioner of the Metropolitan Police, acquiring a knighthood and a wife—the sculptress Judith Raven—on the way.

He first appears in *Death at the President's Lodgings* (1936; US title *Seven Suspects*). Though Appleby may toy with fingerprints and timetables, police routine and procedure are never important, and are never treated with conviction. Indeed, the novels have little connection with reality at all; they are intellectual conceits, in which a complex, logical plot is set against an elaborate, often highly artificial background peopled with eccentric characters, whose conversation is witty, amusing, and erudite, but often irrelevant to the matter at hand. In the earlier novels the author sometimes allows his delight in creating improbable, baroque narrative edifices to get out of hand; and he is inclined to solve difficulties of plot by melodramatic event. As detective stories, the more sober later works are probably to be preferred. In method Innes could be compared with Ellery Queen and John Dickson Carr; he is a better writer than both, however; and an important difference is that he is always concerned to entertain. The detective element is unmistakably there, but it is not absolutely paramount, as it is with Queen and Carr. Appleby himself is somewhat characterless on his first appearance; though he acquires a more definite, individual persona in later works, especially when seen with his wife, at first he is more a mind than a physical presence. His looks are mentioned only as an indication of his social class: the dean of St Anthony's College reflects that Appleby 'was remarkably young, and . . . had all the appearance of being—indeed quite plainly *was*— what Mr Deighton-Clerk still liked to think of under the designation "genteel" '. And again, 'He took another glance at Appleby—the man was indubitably a gentleman.' Appleby exhibits other characteristics of the amateur policeman: he takes pleasure in being wilfully enigmatic, and his speech is stuffed with literary allusions, though he is academically whimsical rather than facetious. Here, for example, is a snatch of conversation with his bucolic colleague Inspector Dodd; its subject is the collection of bones discovered beside the corpse:

Appleby chuckled. 'I see it's the ossuary that really disturbs you. I think it may help a lot.' He picked up a fibula as he spoke and waggled it with professionally excusable callousness at Dodd. And with an association of thought which would have been clear to that efficient officer if only he had been a reader of Sir Thomas Browne he murmured: 'What song the Sirens sang, or what name Achilles assumed when he hid himself among women . . .'

The fibula dropped with a little dry rattle on its pile as Appleby broke off to add: 'Nor is the other question, I hope, unanswerable.'

'*Other* question?'

Whatever their defects as detective stories, the books are always immensely lively, and are written with great charm and wit.

Anne Hocking's (1892–1966) Chief Inspector William Austen, educated at public school and Oxford, 'a tall, military-looking man' who 'dearly loves a classical tag', is another example of the type (*Old Mrs Fitzgerald*, 1939), as is Chief Inspector Roger West, better known as 'Handsome' West, who appears in some forty novels by the incredibly productive John Creasey, beginning with *Inspector West at Home* (1944).

The type is rare among American policemen. However, Lieutenant Michael Lord of the New York Police Department, the detective in C. Daly King's (1895–1963) *Obelists en Route* (1932) and other novels— Lord informs us that he also appeared, under the pseudonym Younghusband, in King's first book, *Obelists at Sea* (1932)—probably belongs here. Described as 'slight and dark, with an alert, questing manner', Lord is otherwise a completely faceless character, who is allowed to bring his powers of ratiocination—which equal those of Ellery Queen—to bear on the problem only towards the end of the narrative. King was a psychologist, and much of these extremely strange novels—the word 'obelist' is given a different definition in each book—is taken up with the theories of psychologists of different schools on the crime. A bibliography of works referred to ends the book, and footnotes assist the reader in comprehending the psychological jargon. A typical example reads: 'The pre-conscious: a most peculiar and Janus-like region. It lies between the conscious and the unconscious, but, so spies report, somewhat closer to the former.'

To Lord can be added three Princeton men. Lieutenant Timothy Trant, casual and flippant, with a 'pleasant, oddly arresting face', is the detective in novels by Q. Patrick—another pseudonym of Hugh Callingham Wheeler, whose books written as Patrick Quentin have already been mentioned (*Death for Dear Clara*, 1937); Dorothy Hughes (b. 1904) writes about one New York detective, Inspector Tobin (*The So Blue Marble*, 1940), and Ruth Fenisong (d. 1978) about another: Sergeant—later Lieutenant, then Captain—Gridley Nelson, who has alienated his ambitious father and snobbish brother by joining the police (*Murder Needs a Name*, 1942).

Like his amateur counterpart, this type of policeman belongs very much to the inter-war years; it was surprising, therefore, when Katharine Farrer (b. 1911) revived the character in 1952 with *The Missing Link*. The title is pleasingly paronomastic, since the plot deals with the abduction of a baby belonging to the Link family, later discovered being suckled by a female ape. Her detective is Inspector Richard Ringwood, an Oxford classical scholar who has abandoned an academic career to go into the police. Like others of his kind, he is undeniably handsome, with 'a lean brown face and rough raven hair', socially more than acceptable, and unrecognizable as a policeman. His Watson is the beautiful blonde Clare Liddicote, whom he later marries. The books have the liveliness and wit of Innes; Ringwood, more active if less ratiocinative than Appleby, shares the latter's taste for literary quotation, while his conversational style echoes that of his remote predecessor Philip Trent. Here he discusses the possibility of an exhumation with Clare and his own bucolic colleague Sergeant Plummer: 'I don't think we're justified in exhuming . . . the public don't like it. . . . Wherefore, they ask (with far less justification than the poet, who really rather enjoyed it), wherefore all this wormy circumstance? why linger at the yawning grave so long? A fair question.'

Ringwood is followed by P. D. James's critically acclaimed policeman Chief Inspector Adam Dalgliesh—this appears to be the correct spelling, although Dalgleish is also found, especially in paperback editions—who makes his entrance in *Cover Her Face* (1962). The characteristics which make him one of this group are neatly brought out in the reactions of the various suspects when they are first introduced to him:

> Catherine Bowers thought, 'Tall, dark and handsome. Not what I expected. Quite an interesting face, really.'
> Stephen Maxie thought, 'Supercilious-looking devil. . . .'
> Eleanor Maxie thought, 'Where have I seen that head before? Of course. That Dürer. In Munich was it? Portrait of an Unknown Man. Why does one always expect police officers to wear bowlers and raincoats?'

These reactions could just as well have been provoked by the appearance of Roderick Alleyn; but there is a vast difference between Ngaio Marsh and P. D. James, in fact. The latter held various posts in hospital administration from 1949 to 1968 and from 1968 to 1979 she was a senior civil servant in the Home Office, working for some time in the criminal policy department. It follows, therefore, that much of the background to her novels, often a hospital or civil service setting, is true to life and detailed—indeed, at times harshly realistic. Nevertheless, she has chosen to give her policeman, however professional he may be in his procedures, the attractiveness and physical appearance of the typical amateur detective; and she compounds this by making him not only a published poet, but also a romantic hero nursing an inner wound—his young wife and their son both died three hours after the child's birth. Despite the accuracy of the settings, the closely knit detection, the sympathetic and convincing character portrayal, however, in the end Dalgliesh lacks verisimilitude as a policeman, if not as a person. Occasionally, too, there is slack and careless detail in the narration. Though the author has written more of Dalgliesh than of her private detective, Cordelia Gray, one cannot help but prefer the latter, even if too sensational, melodramatic moments sometimes jar belief.

Three more senior detectives form a separate subset: Melville Davisson Post's (1869–1930) Sir Henry Marquis (*The Sleuth of St James's Square*, 1920); J. J. Connington's Sir Clinton Driffield (*Murder in the Maze*, 1927); and Anthony Abbot's (pseudonym of Charles Fulton Oursler, 1893–1952) Thatcher Colt (*About the Murder of Geraldine Foster*, 1930; UK title *The Murder of Geraldine Foster*). The three differ from the others in the group in that they all hold superior positions in the police: Sir Henry Marquis is chief of the CID at Scotland Yard, Sir Clinton Driffield the chief constable of an unnamed English county, and Thatcher Colt the police commissioner of New York. All investigate more as amateur detectives than policemen. Marquis, whose exploits are narrated in a series of short stories, rarely works in England, and finds his experiences as the chief of the Secret Service on the borders of the Shan states of more assistance to him than any number of uniformed constables. Colt, the 'most immaculate dresser in the whole city administration', a man 'born to wealth, family and position', carried out personally most of the important investigations during his term of office, but received no credit for them; the balance is now redressed by a series of narratives which, in a device identical to that employed by S. S. Van Dine, purport to be written by his secretary, Anthony Abbot. The most interesting of the three, however, is Connington's Sir Clinton Driffield, who undoubtedly has a claim to be considered among the outstanding detectives of the inter-war years. In his mid-thirties, with sun-tanned face, a firm mouth, and a close-clipped moustache, he is an enthusiastic chess-player and collects books on crime. His Watson is the middle-aged Wendover, a Justice of the Peace, chairman of the County Council, president of the local Antiquarian Society, a 'sort of Ideal Uncle', whom Driffield always addresses as 'Squire', and to whom he is as acerbic as Holmes was to Watson: 'Masterly survey, squire,' said Sir Clinton cordially. 'Except that you've left out most of the points of importance.' When asked at the conclusion of a case to explain his reasoning, he replies with a quotation from *The Hunting of the Snark*, a poem he knows by heart and regularly cites:

> The method employed I would gladly explain
> While I have it so clear in my head
> If I had but the time and you had but the brain—
> But much yet remains to be said.

Wendover is less inclined to hero worship than Watson, however; he often gives as good as he gets, and much of the amusement of the novels comes from the bickerings and disagreements between the unorthodox chief constable and the more conventional, cautious squire. The detection is also excellent, and the scientific detail as well-founded as in Connington's other novels.

The detectives of Joanna Cannan (1898–1961) are hard to categorize. Unlike other authors, she consciously exploits the social inferiority of her policemen to humorous effect, parodying the methods of writers such as Josephine Tey and Ngaio Marsh. When a girl is questioned by Inspector Guy Northeast, for example, rather than being surprised by his gentlemanly aspect, she is disappointed to find that he is not 'quite a gentleman', and later reflects: 'It was a pity that Inspector Northeast was so common' (*They Rang Up the Police*, 1939). Otherwise Northeast is unexceptionable: a large, pleasant, slow young man, third son of a Wiltshire farmer. The author's post-war detective, Inspector Ronald Price, has nothing to recommend him, however (*Murder Included*, 1950; US title *Poisonous Relations*; also in US as *The Taste of Murder*). A socialist suburbanite, at once genteel and vulgar, who drops his aitches, speaks in clichés, and eats with enjoyment 'a substitute for macaroni, covered with a sauce made from dehydrated milk and faintly flavoured with cheese fit for mousetraps', he is, throughout, the butt of the author's remorseless sarcasm (the same hostility, directed at the same social type and the conditions that gave it birth, can be seen in Angela Thirkell's post-war novels). This broad—perhaps too broad—caricature notwithstanding, the characters are subtly and engagingly drawn, the writing is excellent, and the plots ingenious. The author has that rare ability—

the antithesis of sentimentality—to be cruel even to her most attractive characters. Her books certainly deserve to be better known.

FOREIGN POLICEMEN

Whereas foreign amateur and private detectives are extremely rare, foreign policemen crop up with some frequency. A few are naturalized: though of foreign extraction, they belong to an English or American police force. An example is Charlie Chan, the Chinese detective in stories by Earl Derr Biggers (1884–1933), who is a member of the Honolulu Police Department. The vast majority, however, live and work in their own country—Spain and Latin America are the most popular—and result presumably from an author's belief that the tedium of police work can be enlivened by the judicious addition of an intriguing foreign accent or a little local colour, acquired as an expatriate or while on holiday. An additional advantage may be that the foreign detective exists outside the English class system. To these can be added the detectives who are foreign because their authors are. A further class consists of what might be called colonial policemen, the reverse of the Charlie Chan type in a sense: white men investigating crime in various outposts of empire. Finally, there is the very small group of native, or aboriginal, policemen: though they are not foreigners, of course, but just the opposite, it is convenient to treat them here.

The Orient

Charlie Chan, who first appears in *The House without a Key* (1925), was conceived by Biggers as an antipode to the figure of the sinister oriental, a stock character in pulp fiction, and almost immediately achieved immense popularity. Although Biggers wrote only six Chan novels, the character has been used as the basis for innumerable comic strips and radio plays, while forty-seven films—a number exceeded only by Sherlock Holmes—have been made of his exploits. Though extraordinarily fat, Chan walks with 'the light, dainty steps of a woman'. He lives in Honolulu with his wife and eleven children in a bungalow that clings precariously to the slope of Punchbowl Hill. His speech mangles the English language—'Relinquish the firearm, Mr Jennison, or I am forced to make fatal insertion in vital organ belonging to you', for example—and is stuffed with sub-Confucian aphorisms such as 'Bad alibi like dead fish. Cannot stand test of time.'

Amusing and lovable as Chan might be the detection in the novels is not outstanding. The best is probably the first.

Chan has no direct successors, though John P. Marquand's (1893–1960) Mr Moto, Japan's number-one Secret Service agent, obviously owes much to his predecessor (*No Hero*, 1935; UK title *Mr Moto takes a Hand*). Marquand, better known for his novels of New England society, writes well and can weave an adequate plot; but the stories are not crime fiction. Peter Lorre, using very little make-up, brilliantly portrayed Moto in eight films made between 1937 and 1939.

E. V. Cunningham (pseudonym of Howard Fast, b. 1914) uses Chan's example in a different way. His Nisei—Japanese-American—detective, Masao Masuto, is a Zen Buddhist, a karate expert, and a lover of roses who lives with his family in Beverly Hills, where he is a member of the police department. Civilized and cultured, he speaks impeccable English, but can put on a Charlie Chan imitation to disarm suspicion or satisfy racial prejudice. Detection is fair, and the stories are also used as an indictment of the corrupt, wealthy society of Beverly Hills and Los Angeles (*The Case of the One-Penny Orange*, 1977).

Superintendent Tetsuo Otani of the Hyogo Prefectural Police is the detective in a series of novels by James Melville (pseudonym of Roy Peter Martin, b. 1931). The author spent a number of years in Japan as a cultural diplomat, and his deep knowledge of and affection for Japanese life and customs are abundantly evident. At the same time the novels are more than just a guide to Japanese society; in plot and procedure they stand up well against the orthodox police novel (*The Wages of Zen*, 1979).

France

After A. E. W. Mason's Inspector Hanaud there is a considerable gap before the appearance of the next French detective, John Dickson Carr's M. Henri Bencolin, *juge d'instruction* with the Paris police. Bencolin, whose investigations are narrated by a young journalist named Jeff Marle, precedes Carr's other detectives, Fell and Merrivale; but the author's attention is already concentrated on one specific type of murder mystery, the locked-room problem. In *It Walks by Night* (1930), the first Bencolin story, the victim is found beheaded in an empty room without hiding-places, which the murderer could neither have entered nor left, it seems. The improbabilities of the plot are compounded by a highly implausible impersonation scheme.

In 1931 the Belgian novelist Georges Simenon (b. 1903) brought out *M. Gallet décédé* (translated as *The Death of Monsieur Gallet*, US 1932, UK 1933, in *Introducing Inspector Maigret*), the first of a long series of novels in which the detective is Commissaire Jules Maigret of the Paris Police Judiciaire. In the next three years it was followed by eighteen more. Tiring of the character, the author then abandoned him for nearly a decade, but returned to write more than fifty Maigret novels and a number of short stories between 1942 and 1972. Maigret is almost as well known as Sherlock Holmes, and, like Conan Doyle, Simenon has created not only a character, but also an environment. We know of his wife, Madame Maigret, of her cooking, of their much-loved apartment on the Boulevard Richard-Lenoir which they moved into on their marriage, and of the small house in the country at Meung-sur-Loire to which they have retired. We know of Maigret's office in the police headquarters on the Quai des Orfèvres, the only office in the building in which there is still a stove, and we know of his subordinates—Lucas, Janvier, the burly Torrence, and young Lapointe. Yet there is a difficulty: although Maigret is a detective, in name at least, it is not altogether clear that the novels are detective stories. Maigret does not collect evidence, check timetables, break alibis, and finally arrive at solutions through rational deduction. Smoking his pipe, he sits for hours in a sleazy bar or night-club or wanders slowly—almost somnambulistically—through a cheap boarding-house, the rooms of a rich industrialist's mansion, or the corridors and stairways of a grand hotel. Everywhere he imbibes and soaks up the atmosphere, while the answer to the problem gradually ripens and in the end arrives of itself, intuitively. Nor does Maigret view himself as a conventional policeman. In *La première enquête de Maigret* (1948; translated as *Maigret's First Case*, 1958) Simenon tells us something about Maigret's youth: he entered medical school, but left after the death of his father. In fact, the author adds, he never intended to become a real doctor:

. . . the profession he had always wanted to practise did not exist. Even as a young boy, in his village, he had had the impression that many people were in the wrong place, or were going in the wrong direction, simply because they didn't realise it.

And he imagined a man who would be very intelligent and, above all, very understanding, a man who could with a single glance recognize other people's destiny. . . .

This man would be consulted as a doctor is consulted. He would be, to some extent, a repairer of destinies. Not only because he was intelligent. Perhaps he wouldn't need to be exceptionally intelligent? But because he was capable of living the life of all men, of putting himself in the skin of all men.

There is an obvious link between this almost Christ-like ideal and Raymond Chandler's image of the private eye as the perfect man or Ross Macdonald's view of him as a social psychologist whose activities are as much therapeutic as investigative.

Simenon has in fact created a character who is too real for the artificial medium of the detective story. Further, the world Maigret represents, with its real characters and real places, whose various atmospheres are so brilliantly evoked, is one of chance, aleatory, haphazard events, illogical and involuntary, which does not correspond with the neat, logical pattern of life as the detective story sees it. Nevertheless, Simenon has had a considerable influence on the genre. There are more than a few pipe-smoking, ruminative policemen who owe their genesis to Maigret, and whose authors labour, with more or less success, as much upon the creation of an atmosphere as upon the fabrication of a plot.

George Bellairs (pseudonym of Harold Blundell, b. 1902) wrote some fifty books in which the policeman is Inspector—later Superintendent—Thomas Littlejohn. Littlejohn is an obvious imitation of Maigret, and the plots of the novels in which he appears occasionally show some similarity to those of Simenon. The most original of his books are those which take place on the Isle of Man, whose atmosphere Bellairs evokes with some success (*Littlejohn on Leave*, 1941). Alan Hunter's (b. 1922) excellent novels with Superintendent George Gently as the policeman, most of which are set in the author's native East Anglia show a fainter, more controlled influence (*Gently Does It*, 1955), as do W.J. Burley's Superintendent Charles Wycliffe books, whose setting is usually the West Country (*Three-Toed Pussy*, 1968). In Hamilton Jobson's (1914–81) Inspector Anders the influence is even more remote, but still unmistakably there, though this policeman tends to appear only towards the end of the narration, as a kind of physical embodiment of the criminal's conscience (*Therefore I Killed Him*, 1968). Nicolas Freeling (b. 1927) has written, in a quirky and individual style, a number of novels about a Dutch policeman, Inspector Van der Valk, whose attitude to crime and the criminal and view of the policeman's task are very similar to those of Maigret (*Love in Amsterdam*, 1962; US title *Death in Amsterdam*). Perhaps tiring of the character, he killed him off in *A Long Silence* (1972; US title *Auprès de ma Blonde*), replacing him with a French policeman, Henri Castang, a less successful character (*A Dressing of Diamond*, 1974).

Returning to French policemen in general: Commissaire Saturnin Dax of the Paris police appears in novels by Marten Cumberland (1892–1972). In rank and appearance Dax resembles Maigret, but his methods are far more conventional. The author has the agreeable habit of prefacing each chapter with a suitable literary motto (*Someone Must Die*, 1940). Pierre Audemars (b. 1909) has written, in English, of the sensational adventures of Inspector Pinaud of the Sûreté, a lover of good food and wine, fast cars, and beautiful women (*The Two Imposters*, 1958). Equally lacking in seriousness are Mark Hebden's (pseudonym of John Harris, b. 1916) novels set in Burgundy about a less glamorous figure, Chief Inspector Evariste Pel (*Death Set to Music*, 1979).

Spain and Latin America

As might be expected, detective stories set in Spain tend to be by British authors, those set in Latin America by American authors; all are comparatively recent. Bruce Buckingham's (pseudonym of Peter Lilley and Anthony Stansfield) Mexican, Don Francisco de Torla Saavedra, Marqués de Langurén—Don Pancho for short—is the most famous detective in all Latin America, known not only for his skill as an investigator, but also for the fact that, no matter what he is wearing, he always has comfortable Indian huaraches on his feet (*Three Bad Nights*, 1956).

The pleasant husband-and-wife team of Jane and Dagobert Brown, whom we met earlier, was later abandoned—perhaps mistakenly— by their author, Delano Ames, in favour of Juan Llorca, a talkative, amorous corporal who commands the six men of the Civil Guard in Madrigal del Mar, a little village on the Spanish coast. The books are sometimes amusing, with plenty of local colour, but they tend to be overly melodramatic (*The Man in the Tricorn Hat*, 1960).

Suzanne Blanc's Mexican detective, Inspector Miguel Menendes, 'a massive Indian with an immobile face who looks like a grim Aztec idol', is a member of the police department in San Luis, between Monterrey and Mexico City. Impressively erudite and frighteningly intelligent, he despises his sergeant for his stupidity and his wife and mother-in-law for their religious beliefs (*The Green Stone*, 1961).

Brazil is the scene for Robert L. Fish's (1912–81) stories about Captain José da Silva, 'a tall, saturnine man with an aggressive moustache', who is a liaison officer between the Brazilian police and Interpol. He has an amusing Watson, Mr Wilson of the American Embassy; local colour is thick, and the stories are full of action (*The Fugitive*, 1962).

John and Emery Bonnett, whose academic detective, Professor Mandrake, was described earlier, later settled on the Costa Brava and used the district as the setting for stories about the 'violet-eyed', softly spoken Inspector Borges. Again, there is much local colour, which, together with many colourful expatriates, tends to obscure the detection (*Better Dead*, 1964; US title *Better Off Dead*).

Roderic Jeffries (b. 1926), son of Bruce Graeme, continued his father's Blackshirt stories—to be discussed in the next chapter—but, after moving to Mallorca for health reasons, began a series of novels set on the island in which the detective is Inspector Enrique Alvarez. Plots are neat, and local colour restrained. The author is concerned to depict not only the detection, but also the problems brought about by the growth of tourism—in particular, the impact of sudden prosperity on an island population hitherto accustomed to poverty (*Mistakenly in Mallorca*, 1974).

Superintendent Luis Bernal of the Madrid police, an unhappily married, middle-aged man with a distinct resemblance to the late General Franco, is the hero of novels by David Serafin (pseudonym of Ian Michael, b. 1936). The author is professor of Spanish at Oxford, and the books are obviously informed by a deep knowledge of Spanish life, history, and politics. The first were agreeably pure detection, but the more recent books have tended away from this genre towards that of the thriller. The first is *Saturday of Glory* (1979).

Italy

Italian policemen are an even more recent phenomenon. The trend began only in 1980, with Timothy Holme's (1928–87) entertaining novel *The Neapolitan Streak*, in which the detective is the Anglophile Achille Peroni, described as the Rudolph Valentino of the Verona police. A Neapolitan, Peroni hates the north, finding Verona an even more alien environment than London.

Another displaced southerner is Marshal Guernaccia of the

Florentine Carabiniere, the policeman in novels by Magdalen Nabb (b. 1947), who comes from Syracuse, in Sicily. Large and stout, with an eye complaint which compels him to wear dark glasses when the sun shines, Guernaccia is a figure rather in the mould of Maigret. Like the French policeman, he finds atmosphere more important than evidence, and will solve a crime through intuition rather than logic. Florence, where the author lives in what was once the home of Robert and Elizabeth Browning, is extremely well depicted in the novels (*Death of an Englishman*, 1981).

Finally Peter Inchbald has written several novels in which the detective is Inspector Franco Corti, originally of Florence, but now a naturalized UK subject and a member of the art and antiques squad at Scotland Yard (*Tondo for Short*, 1981).

Other countries

Two Australian detectives are S. H. Courtier's (1904–74) Inspector C. J. ('Digger') Haig, a long, lean man with a 'leathery, saturnine, dark-eyed face that seemed to have been pushed violently in different directions' (*Now Seek my Bones*, 1957); and Pat Flower's (1914–78) Detective Inspector Herbert Swinton, who is a much more civilized, home-loving character, with a wife, two children, and an inordinate passion for Australian meat pies (*Wax Flowers for Gloria*, 1958).

H. R. F. Keating (b. 1926) uses India as the setting for his amusing stories about Inspector Ganesh Ghote of the Bombay CID. Ghote is a nervous—not to say timid—man, who must constantly screw up his courage to face, not so much danger, as the possibility of humiliation or social embarrassment. Indeed, the books are an exception among crime novels in that they devote more attention to the detective's state of mind, his doubts, his indecision, and the moral and social dilemmas he faces than to his ratiocinative processes and the solution of the crime. The Indian scene, represented in all its diversity, is remarkably convincing, especially given that Keating visited the country for the first time only ten years after writing the first Ghote novel (*The Perfect Murder*, 1964).

Julian Rathbone (b. 1935), who was for some time an English teacher in Ankara, has used his knowledge of Turkey in a series of very well-written novels—more thrillers than detective stories—in which the hero is Colonel Nur bey, a tall, thin, handsome policeman, who is reputedly incorruptible (*Diamonds Bid*, 1966). In later books Rathbone moved the scene to Spain; and most recently he has set a series of novels—more serious than most crime fiction—in Brabt, a fictional nation in the Low Countries.

The South African town of Trekkersburg in James McClure's (b. 1939) novels is a thin disguise for Pietermaritzburg, in Natal, where the author lived for some twenty years. His policeman is Lieutenant Tromp Kramer, who has a Zulu assistant, Sergeant Zondi. It has been claimed that the books offer a view of the South African system which can stand beside the works of Nadine Gordimer and Alan Paton, but they seem more related to Tom Sharpe's early satires of South African life. Brilliantly funny on occasion, they are also cleverly constructed detective stories (*The Steam Pig*, 1971).

Czechoslovakia is the scene of a series of interconnected short stories by Josef Skvorecky, in which the hero is the blue-eyed, round-faced Lieutenant Josef Boruvka, a detective who differs from most in that the solution of a problem always casts him into a fit of the deepest melancholy. Cunningly constructed, with intricately worked-out murder methods after the classical model, the stories have more than a hint of parody about them (*The Mournful Demeanour of Lieutenant Boruvka*, 1973; originally, as *Smutek porucika Boruvky*, 1966).

Janwillem van de Wetering (b. 1931) once a policeman himself, produced an interesting and serious first novel, *Outsider in Amsterdam* (1976), in which the detectives are sergeants Grijpstra and de Gier of the Dutch police; but later novels degenerate into whimsy and pretentiousness, unfortunately.

Andrew York (pseudonym of Christopher Robin Nicole, b. 1930), who was born in the West Indies, has written several stories set on the fictional Caribbean island of Grand Flamingo. His hero is commissioner of police Colonel Munroe Tallant, formerly a sergeant in the Guyanese police until picked by the premier of Grand Flamingo to command the island's twenty-four-strong police force. The books combine an exotic, authentic setting with a good deal of humour and excitement (*Tallant for Trouble*, 1977).

Inspissated Scandinavian gloom is a feature of the books of two Danes—Poul Ørum (b. 1919), who writes of Inspector Jonas Morck (*The Whipping Boy*, 1972; UK 1975), and Torben Nielsen, whose detective is Superintendent Ancher (*A Gallows-bird's Song*, 1973; UK 1976)—and one Finn—Matti Joensuu, whose Inspector Timo Harjunpaa works in Helsinki. In *Harjunpaa and the Stone Murders* (1986) he gives an infinitely depressing view of teenage delinquency and contemporary urban life in Finland. The Swedish police novels of

Per Wahlöö and Maj Sjöwall are discussed below, in the section on police procedurals.

Colonial policemen

Lawrence G. Blochman, whose Dr Coffee stories have already been mentioned, worked as a journalist in Calcutta during the 1920s, and used his knowledge of India to write a series of novels in which the detective is Inspector Leonidas Prike, 'a dynamic little European' whose 'high-arched skull is as bald as an ostrich egg'. The best-known is probably the first of the series, *Bombay Mail* (1934), in which Prike has to discover which of the suspicious characters travelling on the express from Calcutta to Bombay has murdered the governor of Bengal and stuffed his body into a second-class lavatory. Though the majority of Blochman's characters are Europeans, he writes sympathetically about Indians, and creates a convincing atmosphere.

Much superior, however, in both the quality of the writing and the description of a foreign way of life, are Elspeth Huxley's (b. 1907) novels set in the imaginary East African protectorate of Chania. Though the crimes are confined exclusively to the community of white settlers, the African background, tribal customs, and native beliefs play an important part in the books; indeed, in the first, *Murder at Government House* (1937), the murderer is identified in a witch-doctor's riddle. The detective is Superintendent Vachell, head of the Chania CID, a young Canadian who has come to Africa after a spell first with the Mounties, then with the Indian police.

Frank Arthur (pseudonym of Arthur Frank Ebert, 1902–84), who worked as an accountant in the Fiji Islands during the 1930s, has set several detective novels there. Again, crime is confined to the white community, with the scenery and native population merely forming a backcloth to the action. Arthur's detective is Inspector Spearpoint, a stout figure who in appearance and method resembles Freeman Wills Crofts's Inspector French. At the same time he is very much a character in his own right. The novels are pleasantly readable, and their unusual setting lifts them out of the ruck (*Who Killed Netta Maul?*, 1940; reprinted as *The Suva Harbour Mystery*).

Native policemen

The detectives in this small group, like Hesketh Prichard's November Joe, are kin to the heroes of Fenimore Cooper. Intimate with nature from childhood, they can read the face of the wild with ease. Without peer as trackers, they also know the customs and rituals of the tribe, since they themselves are natives, and can foresee what a fugitive's actions will be.

Arthur W. Upfield (1888–1964), who in 1911 left England for Australia, where he worked as a cook, a boundary rider, an itinerant trapper, and a miner, produced the most famous example of this type of detective when he wrote *The Barakee Mystery* (1929; US title *The Lure of the Bush*) and introduced the 'finest bush detective in the Commonwealth', Inspector Napoleon Bonaparte, a half-caste Australian. 'His features were those of the white man; his complexion was a ruddy black, not the jet-black of the thoroughbred aboriginal.' He is an MA of Brisbane University, and lives outside Brisbane with his wife, also a half-caste, and their three sons. He has an enormous ego and is immensely vain: ' "Having always been interested in lethal weapons, my knowledge of the boomerang is unsurpassed", Bony stated, with unconscious but superb conceit.' Yet, at the same time, he is incredibly charming, and will inveigle acquaintances into discussions on the nature of the universe or the career of Napoleon, whom he considers to be the greatest man who ever lived. Upfield's style is never much better than stiff and wooden, though his dialogue can be lively; but his plots, over-melodramatic in the first novels, improve considerably with time, and some, indeed, are masterly. The outstanding features of the novels, however, are their setting—the Australian outback—and the way in which Bonaparte uses his skills as a tracker and detective to discover clues and draw logical inferences from them.

Tony Hillerman (b. 1925) uses two policemen, both Navajo Indians. Lieutenant Joe Leaphorn of the law and order division polices the 25,000 square miles of the Navajo reservation in Arizona (*The Blessing Way*, 1970); while Sergeant Jim Chee of the Navajo Tribal Police works in New Mexico (*The Dark Wind*, 1983). The scenery of the region—canyon, mesa, and desert—is conjured up effectively, but Hillerman's main interests obviously lie in the religions, cultures, and value systems of the Navajo and Zuñi Indians, subjects which play a large—possibly too large—part in each book. Indeed, it is reported that in the USA the novels are used to teach schoolchildren ethnography.

THE POLICE PROCEDURAL

Even in the inter-war years some authors had begun to deal with the routine of police work, detailing administrative procedures or describing scientific investigations. One such was Sir Basil Thomson, former head of the CID at Scotland Yard, whose police novels have already been mentioned. But these novels and others like them still retained the complex, artificial plot of the detective story. In the 1940s and 1950s, however, there was a gradual trend, partly under the influence of police films and television serials, towards a more naturalistic treatment of police procedures. It followed that detective novels became far more factual than they had been up to this time, and consequently that plots became much simpler and more credible. In place of the murderer who, with immense care and ingenuity, plans and carries out a scheme to baffle the investigator, comes the murderer who kills suddenly in a fit of rage and covers up the traces only clumsily or who attacks an unknown person in the street or robs a liquor store and guns down the proprietor. In other words, for the first time authors appeared to be doing what Raymond Chandler praised Dashiell Hammett for doing—and what he himself did not always do—that is making the murder, its method and its surroundings credible and realistic. At the same time, while in the classical detective story the crime was almost invariably murder, in the new type of police-procedural novel the attempt to imitate reality more closely meant that the crime could be murder, robbery, rape, arson, or fraud—in short, anything which might lead to arrest. Since real policemen often dealt with several crimes at the same time, their fictional counterparts began to find their case-loads increasing. The next step was to show the interlinked activities of several detectives, and after that of a whole police station or precinct. And, as the society with which the policeman had to deal became more brutal and unpleasant, so did art again begin to imitate life. From this brief analysis it might seem as though the police procedural is exclusively an American phenomenon; but, as will become obvious in what follows, this is not the case. It is true that American examples far outnumber British, however, and that not all types of the procedural are represented in British detective fiction.

Lawrence Treat (b. 1903), often called the father of the police procedural, has always disclaimed any intention of creating a new form of detective fiction. Nevertheless, his novels and short stories, beginning with *V as in Victim* (1945), about Lieutenant Bill Decker and detectives Mitch Taylor and Jub Freeman of New York's 21st precinct set a pattern which was to become typical. Its various elements—the character differentiation between the detectives, here the hard-nosed superior, the easygoing, cynical, experienced police-man, and the young, enthusiastic, and idealistic detective; the alternation between the detective at work and the detective at home, where he can be either unhappy, beset with marital problems, or blissfully and sentimentally happy; the perpetually understaffed and overworked squad; the perennial confusion in the squad room; the rivalry between different departments or different policemen; the general hostility of the public—have long ago become clichés of the genre. But Treat's plots still preserve the artificial quality of those of his predecessors.

Though Treat adumbrates many of the qualities of the later police procedural in his books, it seems unlikely that the genre would have developed as rapidly as it did without the influence of radio, televi-sion, and cinema. What was to become the most famous police series of all, *Dragnet*, which related the experiences of Los Angeles police sergeant Joe Friday, began on NBC in 1949, and two years later was transferred to television. The British equivalent, *Z Cars*, set in Liver-pool, ran from 1960 to 1978.

In 1950 MacKinlay Kantor (b. 1904) produced *Signal Thirty-two*, the first of what might be called 'precinct novels'. This was an almost documentary police procedural novel, set in New York's 23rd pre-cinct. Kantor had been given permission by the commissioner of police to accompany patrolmen and detectives as they carried out their work. The result is an extremely realistic novel, in both subject-matter and style. Its other characteristic—and it is this that was taken up by other writers—is that there is no real central figure; the subject is the precinct itself, not a single detective.

The most famous precinct of New York must be the 87th, which appears in a series of novels by Ed McBain (pseudonym of Evan Hunter, b. 1926), beginning with *Cop Hater* (1956). Though a note at the beginning of each volume tells the reader that the novels are set in an 'imaginary city', the setting is obviously New York, with Isola, the borough in which the 87th precinct is located, as Manhattan. Of the detectives in the squad, Steve Carella, who has a beautiful deaf-mute wife, Teddy, is perhaps the most prominent; but all of them— Carella, Meyer Meyer, Cotton Hawes, Bert Kling, Andy Parker, Arthur Brown, Lieutenant Peter Byrnes, and others—can at times play large or small parts and at others be wholly absent from the action, as the plot demands. The early 87th precinct novels are extraordinarily good. McBain had obviously studied police work in detail, and he often included reproductions of the kind of paperwork that passes over a detective's desk—missing person report forms, complaint report forms, resident known criminal cards, scene of the crime sketches—or reproductions of pieces of evidence, thereby adding realism to the narration, while a latent sentimentality was held at bay by a witty, mordant humour. More recent books in the series have been disappointing, however; the plots have become more artificial, and the author makes too frequent use of a Machiavellianly cunning master criminal called the Deaf Man, who sends the detectives cryptic clues to his plans before committing his crimes.

Under her own name in the United States—although under the pseudonym Anne Blaisdell in Britain—Elizabeth Linington writes of the detective squad at Hollywood's Wilcox Avenue police station, where the most prominent member is Sergeant Ivor Maddox (*Greenmask!*, 1964). As Dell Shannon she writes of Lieutenant Luis Mendoza and the Los Angeles Police Department (*Case Pending*, 1960), and as Lesley Egan she chronicles the cases of Vic Varallo and the Glendale Police Department in California (*A Case for Appeal*, 1961). It is obvious that the author has much less firsthand knowledge of police work than Kantor or McBain; nor is it always easy to distinguish between her various detectives, whose home lives are uniformly happy and bland. There is no suggestion, for example, as there very often is in other police-procedural novels, that the demands of police work can place intolerable strain on a marriage. However, the books are all very readable, and Elizabeth Linington succeeds admirably in weaving together in the narrative the threads of a large number of separate, unconnected investigations.

The Swedish co-authors Maj Sjöwall (b. 1935) and Per Wahlöö (1926–75), who were wife and husband, together wrote ten novels about a Stockholm police squad led by Inspector—later Superintendent—Martin Beck: the first is *Roseanna* (1965; translated 1967). They were both Communists, and the aim of the series was, as they wrote, echoing Godwin, to 'use the crime novel as a scalpel cutting open the belly of an ideologically pauperized and morally debatable so-called welfare state of the bourgeois type'. The first few books were designed to be untendentious, but the political element was to increase gradually, reaching a climax in the final book—as indeed it does. *The Terrorists* (1975; translated 1976) is a violent attack on right-wing dictatorships, American imperialism, and Sweden's fake socialist society, a welfare state which 'abounds with sick, poor and lonely people, living at best on dog food'. It ends with Beck's former colleague Lennart Kollberg beginning a word-game with the remark: 'My turn to start? Then I say X—X as in Marx.' However irritating and one-sidedly tendentious the political element may be, the books—particularly the early ones—are impressive as police procedurals. Police routine is well researched and realistic, though the plots are often over-elaborate. Depiction of character is deeper and more subtle than in McBain or Linington, and the principal figures are allowed to change and develop in the course of the series. Yet there is an ambiguity about the authors' attitude to their characters, which stems from their ideological stance, and which makes the books very uneven in tone. At times the police are treated as inefficient buffoons who are incapable of doing a single thing right, and the books turn into knockabout farce. At other times the police are viewed as honest, decent people who are doing their best at a difficult and degrading job, in which case a proper seriousness is brought to bear on the subject. The result of this unevenness, however, is to confuse the reader, and to spoil the books as a series.

In Britain Roger Busby (b. 1941), for a long time the crime-reporter on a Birmingham newspaper, produced *Robbery Blue* (1969), a police procedural set in an imaginary Midlands city which tells of a hunt for criminals who have robbed a security van and killed a policeman. Detective Sergeant Leric, in this novel a hidden alcoholic, is later promoted and becomes the central figure of a series.

Undoubtedly the most individual of all police procedurals is William Marshall's (b. 1944) series about the Yellowthread Street police station in Hong Kong (*Yellowthread Street*, 1975). Though in manner they have a certain similarity to McBain's novels, they go much beyond them, becoming almost surrealistic at times. A more important influence on Marshall has been Chester Himes, whose equally surreal Harlem detective stories are mentioned below. Marshall's usual method is to begin with an extraordinary, seemingly lunatic situation—in *The Far Away Man* (1984), for example, all the victims of the killer are carrying cholera vaccination certificates which are not their own—which, on investigation, proves to be susceptible of a perfectly reasonable explanation. The action is always incredibly fast and frenetic, and often hilariously funny. Marshall's narration and prose are so energetic that occasionally they miss the target completely, but at their best the novels have a verve and crackle which is hard to find elsewhere.

More recently Peter Turnbull has begun a police-procedural series about a squad of Glasgow detectives—*Deep and Crisp and Even* (1981) is the first. These are tougher and grittier than most, but not without a redeeming streak of humour. Turnbull may turn out to be Glasgow's McBain, though his policemen are not sufficiently individualized as yet.

Meanwhile a more conventional type of police procedural, in which the action revolves around an individual rather than a precinct, station, or squad, had been developing in Britain. Maurice Proctor (1906–73), who spent nineteen years in the police in the north of England, put his experience to good use in over twenty-five police novels. He has two detectives: Detective Superintendent Philip Hunter (*The Chief Inspector's Statement*, 1951; US title *The Pennycross Murders*), who works in Yoreborough, a medium-sized, northern town which might easily be York; and Detective Chief Inspector Harry Martineau (*Hell is a City*, 1954; US title *Somewhere in This City*; in US also as *Murder Somewhere in This City*), who is a member of the CID in Grantchester, which is described as the 'Metropolis of the North' and is probably based on Manchester. Both series are good, but the best of the Martineau novels are outstanding. Proctor not only knows how the police work; he is also able to re-create the atmosphere of the office, the canteen, and the interrogation room. Though there is some use of the police laboratory, in the main Martineau is an old-fashioned policeman who obtains his results through careful, painstaking investigation and questioning. But he has flair as well; and in his instinctive, empathetic understanding of what has happened, he is not unlike Maigret.

A few months after the appearance of Martineau the prolific John Creasey, writing as J. J. Marric, produced *Gideon's Day* (1955; US title *Gideon of Scotland Yard*), the first in a series of twenty-one books—probably Creasey's best work—about Commander George Gideon of Scotland Yard. Gideon has Maigret's physical bulk and presence, as well as his sympathy for the little criminal caught up in events beyond him. But the main features of the series are the authentic background, the simultaneous investigation of several cases, and the alternation between Gideon's work as a policeman and his home life: unlike Linington, Creasey neither overdoes nor sentimentalizes the domesticity.

Some years later Eric Bruton (b. 1915) took the City of London police as the basis for a series of police procedurals, using Moor Lane police station, demolished in the war, as the setting. His central figure is Detective Inspector George Judd, head of the CID of 'A' division, a big man with a cropped, black, handlebar moustache and the flattened nose of a boxer. These are workmanlike stories, with a good London setting (*The Laughing Policeman*, 1963).

In America Ben Benson (1915–59) took the procedural out of the city with his novels about Inspector Wade Paris (*Beware the Pale Horse*, 1951) and trooper Ralph Lindsay (*The Venus Death*, 1953) of the Massachusetts State Police. Like McBain, he often includes facsimiles of police documents in the books and keeps several investigations going at the same time. He has been followed by Hillary Waugh (b. 1920), who in 1952 published one of the best police novels so far written, *Last Seen Wearing* . . ., which follows the dogged, painstaking investigation of two Massachusetts police-officers in their attempt to track down Marilyn Mitchell, a pretty 18-year-old who has vanished from college. Waugh did not use the detectives of this novel again, but in *Sleep Long, My Love* (1959; in UK also as *Jigsaw*) he introduced Fred Fellows, chief of police in the imaginary Connecticut town of Stockford. A large man with a paunch, Fellows gives the superficial impression of a simple countryman with a penchant for pointless anecdotes. In fact, he is not only a good policeman who is thoroughly conversant with modern methods; he also has something in common with the native detective: he has a feeling for nature, and his hunches tend to be more those of the tracker than those of the trained policeman. Unlike most characters of this type, Fellows does not occupy a dominating position in the narrative; Waugh moves the point of view around, from suspect to suspect, policeman to policeman. He often likes to begin a novel with a prologue in which the crime is committed, or the events leading up to the crime occur; but the books are so good that the use of this melodramatic, over-employed device can be forgiven.

Other policemen who are used as central figures in police procedurals include Joseph Harrington's (b. 1903) Francis X. Kerrigan of the New York Police Department, who, when we first meet him, has been busted down from lieutenant to sergeant (*The Last Known Address*, 1965). Kerrigan, an older, experienced policeman, takes Jane Boardman, a pretty, young, college-educated beginner under his wing, and the development of the relationship between them is well done, as is the tedious routine of investigation. Collin Wilcox (b. 1924) writes novels about Lieutenant Frank Hastings of the San

Francisco police. Though the routine of the investigation is still there, Wilcox tends to involve Hastings personally in his cases. In the first, *The Lonely Hunter* (1969), for example, Hastings's daughter runs away and becomes entangled in an intrigue of murder and drug dealing in the Haight-Ashbury district of San Francisco. This characteristic takes the stories, good though they are, out of the police-procedural class. Rex Burns's (b. 1935) novels about Detective Gabriel Wager, a Chicano who works in the organized crime division of the Denver police, are more conventional (*The Alvarez Journal*, 1975). Burns does the background, the nuts and bolts of police procedure, very well, even providing a glossary of acronyms met with in the text: for example, DALE stands for Office of Drug Abuse Law Enforcement, WATS for Wide Area Telecommunications Services. The conversational idiom is convincingly authentic. And in the contrast between Wager and his partner Denby, Burns makes a point about police work which is fundamental to the police procedural. Of himself Wager thinks: 'He had lousy pay, an insecure job, and hours longer than a whore's Saturday night, but it was his own time and that made all the difference.' And of Denby: 'Denby had a wife and a new kid, a home and probably a cat or a dog. Family. Liked to take his wife to the movies. Deep down, liked to have her tell him what to do. Wager didn't think Denby would last long in the narcotics squad.'

Policewomen are relatively rare as central figures. The earliest example is English, but she appears to have been conceived as an equivalent of the tough American investigator of the 1930s. This is Nigel Morland's (1905–86) Miss Palmyra Pym, a hard-bitten woman famous for her hats who holds the rank of deputy assistant commissioner at Scotland Yard. She is hardly a serious character: on her first appearance, in *The Phantom Gunman* (1935), she routs a gang of American criminals with a Thompson sub-machine-gun. More realistic are two New York policewomen, Dorothy Uhnak's (b. 1933) Christie Opara (*The Bait*, 1968) and Lillian O'Donnell's (b. 1926) Norah Mulcahaney (*The Phone Calls*, 1972). Dorothy Uhnak worked for the New York City Transit Police for fourteen years; in an autobiographical work, *Policewoman: A Young Woman's Initiation into the Realities of Justice* (1964), she describes some of her experiences. Her novels are an attempt to initiate readers into this reality. Though she is no stylist, it is impossible not to be drawn into her powerful, harsh, violent narratives. Lillian O'Donnell has greater skill as a novelist, but there is little of the police procedural about her books. The plots are conventional and artificial, and the heroine's—it is significant that this noun comes naturally to mind—family life is given a disproportionate amount of space.

Though Joseph Wambaugh (b. 1937) has produced no series detective, his novels cannot be omitted from a discussion of the police procedural. The author was in the Los Angeles Police Department for fourteen years, and the background to his novels could not be more authentic. In the best of them—*The Choirboys* (1975) and *The Delta Star* (1983)—he combines harsh, realistic brutality and obscenity with hilarious farce, rather in the manner of the television series *Hill Street Blues*, which seems likely to have been influenced in its conception by his novels. The British equivalent to Wambaugh is possibly James Barnett, whose first novel, *Head of the Force* (1978), begins with the discovery of the commissioner of the Metropolitan Police sitting at his desk in Scotland Yard, his severed head in front of him, impaled on the spike of a ceremonial dress helmet of the now defunct Glamorgan Constabulary. In later novels the author moves away from the police procedural, however, and stretches credibility to the limit as his detective, Chief Superintendent Owen Smith, is first drawn into Intelligence work and later finds himself resisting an attempt at world domination.

OTHER AMERICAN POLICEMEN

During the inter-war years police detectives were relatively rare in American fiction: not only were they overshadowed by the private eye, but they also had to live down the reputation they had previously acquired for stupidity, inefficiency, and corruption. It is perhaps because of this reputation that Rufus King (1893–1966) makes his detective, Lieutenant Valcour of the New York Police Department, French-Canadian rather than Irish, as would have been more probable. Valcour, a mild, elderly man, drags out a series of interminable investigations which have little to recommend them (*Murder by the Clock*, 1929). Helen Reilly's (1891–1962) novels about Inspector Christopher McKee, head of the Manhattan homicide squad, who is continually referred to as 'the Scotsman', as though he were a train, were once popular, but have sadly faded (*The Diamond Feather*, 1930). More interesting are the stories by Lange Lewis (pseudonym of Jane Lewis Benton, b. 1915) set in Los Angeles, in which the detective is Inspector Richard Tuck (*Murder among Friends*, 1972).

Margaret Millar, Ross Macdonald's wife, who has already been mentioned as the author of several novels with a psychiatrist-detective, also wrote two novels in which Inspector Sands of the Toronto Police Department appears. Described as a 'thin, tired-looking middle-aged man with features that fitted each other so perfectly that few people could remember what he looked like', Sands plays the part of an observer, rather than a detective (*Wall of Eyes*, 1943). A much more conventional Canadian detective—though a far more recent one—is Inspector Charlie Salter, whose professional and domestic problems are catalogued by Eric Wright in *When the Gods Smiled* (1983).

Chester Himes (1909–84) was an unsuccessful black writer living in Paris when a French publisher suggested that he write a thriller set in Harlem. The result, *La Reine des Pommes* (1958; translated as *For Love of Imabelle*, 1959; also as *A Rage in Harlem*), won the Grand Prix Policier that year, and was followed by nine more 'Harlem domestic detective stories', as Himes ironically termed them. All except one originally appeared in French, and all except two have as heroes two black detectives, Coffin Ed Johnson and Gravedigger Jones. Written with great verve and panache, they are at once exceedingly violent and exhilaratingly comic. They are full of surreal—almost hallucinatory—incidents, and most of the characters, including the two policemen, are far larger than life. But the books have a more serious side: indeed, one critic has said that Himes's Harlem is like a picture by Hieronymus Bosch. As the series progresses, the detectives become more weary and cynical. Himes apparently wanted to end the series with a novel in which the two policemen would be killed trying to prevent a black revolution. 'But I had to stop. The violence shocks even me', he wrote.

A more conventional black detective is John Ball's (b. 1911) Virgil Tibbs of the Pasadena Police Department, who first appears in *In the Heat of the Night* (1965). Pharoah [sic] Love is a black homosexual policeman in New York in George Baxt's (b. 1923) *A Queer Kind of Love* (1966); but neither the police work nor the homosexual scene have much semblance of reality.

One of the most interesting of recent American writers is K. C. Constantine (a pseudonym), who has written a number of novels set in the fictional small town of Rocksburg in western Pennsylvania, a coal-mining town with no coal left. His detective is the town's police chief, the 'half-hunkie, half-dago'—in other words, Serbo-Italian—

Mario Balzic. Plots and detection are more than adequate, but the real attraction of the novels is the quality of the writing. The author has a wonderful ear for the varieties and nuances of demotic American speech, and reproduces them sharply and funnily. Balzic himself is a superbly drawn character who occupies the centre of the stage throughout; the novels are as much about him—his memories, his coming to terms with the past, his relations with his family and colleagues—as they are about crime and detection—*The Rocksburg Railroad Murders* (1972) is the first.

OTHER BRITISH POLICEMEN

After the war the distinctions between the various categories of policemen become blurred, and, perhaps as a consequence, the policemen themselves tend to lose individuality. This is not true of some of the earlier examples: for instance, L. A. G. Strong (1896–1958), the poet and novelist, wrote several stories about Inspector Ellis McKay of Scotland Yard, who is also a composer, the 'West Highland Rhapsody' being one of his works. McKay, with his 'thick, sturdy figure, cheerful rubicund face with prominent blue eyes, and high forehead topped by tufts of reddish hair that stood up round a large bald patch like furze round a clearing', is a distinctive and individual figure; the novels are marked, too, by pleasant by-play between McKay and his provincial colleague Inspector Bradstreet (*All Fall Down*, 1944).

Equally individual, if in a different way, is Patrick Petrella of the Metropolitan Police, who, in a series of short stories by Michael Gilbert written in the 1950s and 1960s, progresses from constable to detective chief inspector. Son of a Spanish policeman and an English schoolmistress, he can speak four languages, including Arabic, is a skilled lock-picker, and has a sound knowledge of wines. The stories are collected in *Petrella at Q* (1977) and *Young Petrella* (1988).

Others are less well defined. Inspector Burnival, in novels by Edward Candy (pseudonym of Barbara Alison Neville, b. 1925), is 'a short, undistinguished figure' with 'small, predatory features', but is otherwise unremarkable. The role of eccentric detective is taken over by a Father Christmas-like figure, Professor Fabian Honeychurch, an eminent paediatrician who acts as Burnival's Watson (*Which Doctor?*, 1953). Not much is known of Nigel Fitzgerald's Superintendent Duffy other than that he comes from Dublin (*Midsummer Malice*,

1953) or of Gwendoline Butler's (b. 1922) Inspector Coffin other than
that he is self-educated and works at a police station in south London
(*Dead in a Row*, 1957). Her policewoman, Charmian Daniels, about
whom she writes under the name of Jennie Melville, has more individuality: she has yellow hair and big brown eyes, was born in
Dundee, took a degree in social science at Glasgow University, has
mapped out her career, and is fighting her way up through the police
hierarchy (*Come Home and Be Killed*, 1962).

Mary Kelly's (b. 1927) Inspector Brett Nightingale (*A Cold Coming*, 1956) is distinguished by the possession of a Jaguar XK sports car;
the novels in which he appears are adventures rather than detective
stories, while John Austwick's (pseudonym of Austin Lee, 1904–65)
Inspector Parker seems fated to spend his time solving murders that
have occurred in public libraries (*Murder in the Borough Library*,
1959).

Detective Superintendent Bradbury and his assistant, Detective
Sergeant Christopher Raymond, the detectives in novels by Norman
Longmate (b. 1925) are a pleasantly old-fashioned pair, whose lei-
surely investigation is well narrated (*A Head for Death*, 1958). The
same is true of Elizabeth Lemarchand's (b. 1906) detectives,
Detective Superintendent Tom Pollard and Gregory Toye (*Death of
an Old Girl*, 1967).

John Buxton Hilton's (1921–86) Superintendent Simon Kenworthy,
'deceptively sleepy, flippant and cynical at times', is subtly
portrayed—too subtly, perhaps, for just as he is often misunderstood
by his subordinates, so he is likely to suffer the same fate at the hands
of his readers (*Death of an Alderman*, 1968). Jonathan Ross's (b. 1916)
Detective Superintendent George Rogers is a much simpler character,
with a lecherous streak which can lead him into trouble (*The Blood
Running Cold*, 1968). Roy Lewis's (b. 1933) Inspector John Crow is
memorable for his height and cadaverous physique (*A Lover Too
Many*, 1969), and Pauline Glen Winslow's Superintendent Capricorn
for the fact that he used to be a magician (*Death of an Angel*,
1975).

Douglas Clark (b. 1919), reverting to pre-war models, uses differences in class and education to set up hostility between his two
detectives. Detective Chief Inspector George Masters is an erudite
intellectual, a high flyer at the Yard, who resents being given Inspector Green, whom he considers a 'passed-over old has-been', as his
assistant. Green returns the dislike, but over the course of several

books the two gradually become trusted colleagues and close friends (*Nobody's Perfect*, 1969).

PROVINCIAL POLICEMEN

The traditional opening moves in the police detective story are: a body is discovered; the local police are called in; after an initial investigation they realize that the crime is too complex or their resources too limited to deal with it and, reluctantly, they send a summons to Scotland Yard. With the arrival of a Roderick Alleyn figure the overture ends, and the first act begins. The advantage of this method is obvious. It avoids the humdrum small town or county atmosphere, and makes it possible to place the same detective in a great variety of different settings without overstepping the bounds of credibility. More recently, however, a number of authors have begun to use the opposite approach, purposely courting, as it were, the humdrum. By retaining the same setting in a series of books, they have been able to give their work a more recognizably regional flavour; at the same time their detective acquires roots, individuality, and a well-defined position in local society. Overall, the result is a gain in realism.

Gil North (pseudonym of Geoffrey Horne, b. 1916) began the trend with *Sergeant Cluff Stands Firm* (1960). Detective Sergeant Caleb Cluff is a policeman in the little Yorkshire town of Gunnarshaw, which appears to be based on the author's native town of Skipton. Middle-aged, the son of a local farmer, he lives in a cottage a few miles outside the town with his cat and sheepdog, Clive. He wears heavy tweeds and a shapeless tweed hat with a grouse feather in the band, and carries a thick, chestnut-wood walking-stick. There is little detection of the usual sort, and the stories are narrated in an odd, almost impressionistic prose, and an elliptic, allusive manner. Nevertheless, Cluff is established as a distinctive, original character, and both he and the setting have a strong, undeniably Yorkshire flavour. The flavour is less marked in Reginald Hill's (b. 1936) novels, which are set in a more urban Yorkshire, but it is still unmistakably there. These have, however, a much stronger detective element, and Hill's two policemen—the fat, coarse, brutal Superintendent Andrew Dalziel and the young, liberal-minded, university-educated Sergeant Peter Pascoe, who later marries an ardent feminist—make an impressive, interesting team (*A Clubbable Woman*, 1970).

In general, other regions have not produced such colourful characters; nor is the sense of locality so pronounced. Ruth Rendell's (b. 1930) acclaimed series of novels in which the detective is Chief Inspector Reginald Wexford take place in Sussex (*From Doon with Death*, 1964), while June Thomson's (b. 1930) Inspector Finch (called 'Inspector Rudd' in the USA) is a policeman in Essex (*Not One of Us*, 1971). Sheila Radley's (pseudonym of Sheila Mary Robinson, b. 1928) Chief Inspector Douglas Quantrill works in Suffolk (*Death and the Maiden*, 1978), and Dorothy Simpson's (b. 1933) Inspector Thanet, as his name suggests, in Kent (*The Night She Died*, 1981). All are well portrayed, as are their colleagues, their wives and children, and their domestic background generally. Though this gives them a distinct individuality at the time of reading, on looking back the outlines tend to become indistinct, and it is difficult to distinguish one from another.

The success of Colin Dexter (b. 1930), whose beer-drinking Chief Inspector Morse lives and works in Oxford—not the academic Oxford of Crispin, Innes, or Masterman; the town, rather than the gown—suggests that the use of a specific place—and the more numinous the place, the better—is more conducive to the creation of a local atmosphere than the use of an area, a region or a county (*Last Bus to Woodstock*, 1975). The novels of S. T. Haymon, in which Inspector Benjamin Jurnet investigates cases in and around a city which is recognizably Norwich, tend to bear this view out—*Death and the Pregnant Virgin* (1980) is the first.

A final member of this group might be Catherine Aird (pseudonym of Kim Hamilton McIntosh, b. 1930), who has written a number of novels set in the fictional county of Calleshire in which the detective is Inspector C. D. Sloan (*The Religious Body*, 1966). They are nicely contrived and pleasantly unpretentious, but it is difficult to create a sense of place with an imaginary locality, and Calleshire, which appears to be based on Kent, is unfortunately no Barsetshire.

Chapter 5

A FEW ODDITIES

> 'Well, my boy, what do you make of this lot?' he asked, smiling at my expression.
>
> 'It is a curious collection.'
>
> 'Very curious, and the story that hangs round it will strike you as being more curious still.'
>
> (A. Conan Doyle, 'The Adventure of the Musgrave Ritual')

COMEDY

The tone of the crime novel is essentially serious; hardly surprising for a genre on whose periphery lurk works such as *Crime and Punishment* and *Dr Jekyll and Mr Hyde*. The detective story is generally a far more light-hearted affair, which never forgets for long that its primary aim is to entertain. The facetiousness of Trent and Wimsey, the wise-cracks of Philip Marlowe and Archie Goodwin, the wit and humour of Edmund Crispin, Michael Innes, and Cyril Hare, are all tolerated within the detective story; more than that, they form an integral part of it. A number of writers have gone further, however, and, making humour the dominant element, have produced comic detective stories.

Comedy can be achieved in a number of ways; perhaps the simplest is to turn the detective or policeman into a comic figure. George Bagby's (pseudonym of Aaron Marc Stein, b. 1906) Inspector Schmidt, chief of Manhattan's homicide squad, is troubled constantly by aching feet, and can only think rationally after taking off his shoes and donning a pair of slippers. The novels, beginning with *Murder at the Piano* (1935), purport to be narrated by Bagby, a journalist who acts as Schmidt's Watson. Joyce Porter (b. 1924) has written a number of novels—the first is *Dover One* (1964)—in which the detective is Chief Inspector Wilfred Dover of Scotland Yard. Dover is gross, mean, greedy, rude, and incompetent. A similar character, less fat but more stupid, is Jack S. Scott's (pseudonym of Jonathan Escott, b. 1922) provincial policeman, Inspector Rosher, who, with his brown teeth and Anthony Eden hat, is an embarrassment to both his superiors and his subordinates (*The Poor Old Lady's Dead*, 1976). Though both these authors produce good stories and good detection, their monstrous characters soon pall.

Other writers have parodied the genre: Julian Symons's (b. 1912) first novel, *The Immaterial Murder Case*, written in 1936 but not published until 1945, has a self-opinionated amateur detective called Teak Woode, who is, as his name suggests, impenetrably thick-witted. The policeman, Inspector Bland, is a more normal figure who appears again in two later novels by Symons. In his memoirs, *Notes from Another Country* (1972), the author calls it a 'fairly dotty' story, 'appallingly bad' in terms of plot. Its main interest lies in its carica-tures of literary figures of the 1930s, most obviously of the poet Ruthven Todd, whose own detective novels have already been men-tioned, and in the felicitous invention of Immaterialism, an art movement whose practitioners paint what is not there, not material. In Leo Bruce's first Sergeant Beef novel, *Case for Three Detectives* (1936), Lord Simon Plimsoll, Monsieur Amer Picon, and Monsignor Smith, whose originals are not hard to discern, fail to solve the mystery and are worsted by the red-faced, bucolic Sergeant Beef, to whom the murderer has been obvious from the outset. The book is amusing, and contains some telling thrusts at the absurdity of the amateur detective's behaviour. 'My knowledge of these situations, gathered from some study of them', remarks the narrator,

'taught me that we were all behaving according to the very best precedents, but I could not help feeling that a man who had just lost his wife might not see it that way. I had learnt that after a murder it is quite proper and conven-tional for everyone in the house to join the investigators in this entertaining game of hide-and-seek which seemed wholly to absorb us. It was not extra-ordinary for there to be three total strangers questioning the servants, or for the police to be treated with smiling patronage, or for the corpse to be pulled about by anyone who was curious to know how it had become a corpse.

A similar type of parody, but less successful and less caustic, is Marion Mainwaring's *Murder in Pastiche, or Nine Detectives All at Sea* (1954), in which a murder on a liner sailing from Liverpool to New York is investigated by Trajan Beare, Spike Bludgeon, Mallory King, Sir Jon. Nappleby, Jerry Pason, Atlas Poireau, Lord Simon Quinsey, Miss Fan Silver, and Broderick Tourneur.

Comic situation, often combined with farcical plot and inept detective, usually results in novels which may be funny but have little to do with detection. Among the comic extravaganzas written by Caryl Brahms (pseudonym of Doris Caroline Abrahams, 1901–82) and S. J. Simon—of which the best is undoubtedly *No Bed for Bacon* (1941)—are four which could be termed detective stories, although Inspector Adam Quill, who constantly consults his *Detective's Handbook*, seldom solves a case. It is the mixture of running gags, parody, allusions, exaggerated characters, and knockabout farce which makes them amusing and highly readable (*A Bullet in the Ballet*, 1937). Elliott Paul's (1891–1958) series of novels set in Paris, in which the hero-detective is Homer Evans, an irresponsible but brilliant playboy and artist, have worn less well, though there is still some amusement to be derived from the satiric portrayal of pre-war artistic life on the Left Bank (*The Mysterious Mickey Finn; or, Murder at the Café du Dôme*, 1939).

Nancy Spain (b. 1917) wrote a number of comic detective stories with a variety of settings. *Poison in Play* (1945), the first, is set at Wimbledon during the all-England tennis championship, while others take place at a Swiss ski resort, an expensive girls' school, and on board a cruise liner. In the majority the detective is Miriam Birdseye, 'tall, and thin and blonde and not very handsome', a performer in intimate revues whose ambition is to play Ibsen. Though the books are ignored by reference works on the detective story, they are worth seeking out, as are Peter Antony's (pseudonym of Anthony and Peter Shaffer, both b. 1926) three novels written in the 1950s in which the detective is Mr Verity—in the third, his name becomes Fathom—who is a 'bearded giant, ruthless inquirer, devastating wit, and enthusiastic collector of the best sculpture'. The first, *The Woman in the Wardrobe* (1951), is not only extremely funny; it is also a brilliant variant on the locked-room problem.

More forced in humour are Michael Kenyon's (b. 1931) Irish detective stories with a Dublin policeman, Superintendent O'Malley, whose investigations are occasionally assisted by premonitory dreams (*The 100,000 Welcomes*, 1970), and Tim Heald's (b. 1944) novels about Simon Bognor, a greedy, somewhat stupid special investigator from the Board of Trade (*Unbecoming Habits*, 1973).

The most successful comic detective stories are undoubtedly the series of novels by Colin Watson (1920–83) set in Flaxborough, an imaginary little town in East Anglia 'with the oddest jumble of house-tops you ever saw and a pub and a church every twenty yards', once described by a local inhabitant as 'a high-spirited town . . . like Gomorrah' (*Coffin, Scarcely Used*, 1958). In successive novels the author gradually assembles a solid cast of characters: Harcourt Chubb, the vacuous-minded chief constable, with his Yorkshire terrier-breeding wife; Amblesby, the coroner, described by a former mayor as one of the 'venereal institutions of this ancient town'; Dr Heinemann, the pathologist, and Inspector Purbright, the detective throughout the series. Quiet, amiable, and unassuming, Purbright is the only character who is not, to some extent, a caricature; it is he who holds the novels together and is at the same time a convincing and efficient detective. Extraordinarily funny, in both plot and narration, the books also turn a sharply satirical eye on modern British society.

HISTORY

Though the practice of setting detective stories in the past—an obvious extension of the wish to make the detective and his surroundings as colourful as possible—is on the whole comparatively recent, the first example dates back to 1918, when Melville Davisson Post published a collection of short stories entitled *Uncle Abner, Master of Mysteries*. Abner, an austere, deeply religious man of absolute integrity and moral grandeur, lives in the mountainous hinterland of Virginia in the decades preceding the Civil War; he has no official position, but believes that, in 'a world filled with the mysterious justice of God'—which he, like Father Brown, infinitely prefers to the laws of man—his mission is to bring about the divine will. He is undeniably an impressive, powerful figure with no mean skills as a detective; and, again like Father Brown, he tends to express himself enigmatically and paradoxically.

Nearly thirty years later Lillian de la Torre (pseudonym of Lillian McCue, b. 1902) used a real historical personage, Samuel Johnson, as her detective in a series of short stories, later collected into two volumes, of which the first is *Dr Sam: Johnson, Detector* (1946). The stories purport to be narrated by Boswell, and the author strikes the latter's tone admirably: as literary-historical pastiche they are extremely successful, but rather less convincing as detection.

In 1949 Robert H. van Gulik (1910–67), a Dutch diplomat and sinologist, brought out *Dee Goong An*, a translation of part of an anonymous eighteenth-century Chinese novel, which relates three cases solved by Judge Dee (630–700), a famous statesman of the Tang dynasty. He followed this by a number of original novels written in English in which Judge Dee, usually in the role of a district magistrate, is the detective and central figure—the first is *The Chinese Maze Murders* (1959). The novels follow the tradition of the Chinese detective story in having three separate, but interwoven, plots. Some episodes are mildly supernatural, and there is much detail relating to Chinese life and customs, although it has been pointed out that the picture is of a generalized medieval China, rather than of the China of the Tang period. Though very unlike the conventional detective story, van Gulik's novels are undeniably interesting and well told.

For the author who intends to write a historical detective story, the Victorian era is probably the most attractive. Different from, yet at the same time not altogether dissimilar to, present-day society, it is, through the existence of Holmes and his contemporaries, the classical background. Peter Lovesey (b. 1936) has made very good use of the setting in a series of Victorian police novels in which the detective is the lean Sergeant Cribb, assisted by the stout Constable Thackeray; the first, *Wobble to Death* (1970), takes place at one of the six-day endurance contests popular in the 1880s. Ray Harrison's novels about two members of the City of London police, Sergeant Bragg and Constable Morton, who also plays cricket for England, are set a few years later (*French Ordinary Murder*, 1983), while Francis Selwyn (b. 1935), who writes of the portly Sergeant William Clarence Verity, places his novels earlier, in the London of the 1850s (*Cracksman on Velvet*, 1974; also as *Sergeant Verity and the Cracksman*). Finally, John Buxton Hilton uses Victorian and Edwardian rural Derbyshire as the setting for several stories in which the detective is Inspector Thomas Brunt (*Rescue from the Rose*, 1976).

The most successful historical detective, however, as far as popularity goes, must be the twelfth-century monk Caedfel, the former crusader who now tends the herb garden at the Benedictine abbey at Shrewsbury, the series character in a long series of novels by Ellis Peters (pseudonym of Edith Mary Pargeter, b. 1913)—the first is *A Morbid Taste for Bones* (1977). The medieval background is exceedingly well done, as is the detection in the earlier volumes of the series. Latterly, however, romance appears to have taken over.

CROOKS AND VILLAINS

During the first period of the detective story, the years between the first appearance of Sherlock Holmes and the end of the First World War, crooks of various kinds, oddly enough in decades which in retrospect seem the acme of social stability, were no less popular heroes—or at least central figures—of detective stories than the detective or policeman himself.

Conan Doyle had popularized the figure of the Napoleon of crime with the character of Professor Moriarty, the mathematical genius who 'sits motionless, like a spider in the centre of its web', the 'organiser of half that is evil and nearly all that is undetected' in London. He is followed by Guy Boothby's (1867–1905) Dr Nikola, a sinisterly handsome, ruthless character with hypnotic powers, who is accompanied everywhere by a huge, malevolent black cat (*A Bid for Fortune, or Dr Nikola's Vendetta*, 1895). A little later Sax Rohmer (pseudonym of Arthur Henry Sarsfield Ward, 1883–1959) created the first, and possibly the best, of the sinister oriental villains: Dr Fu Manchu, a diabolical fiend whose schemes to make himself emperor of the world are constantly thwarted by the efforts of Sir Denis Nayland Smith, a noted orientalist, and his friend Dr Petrie (*The Mystery of Dr Fu-Manchu*, 1913). Later in his career, however, Fu Manchu loses his interest and our affection when he supinely allows himself to be persuaded to abandon his plans for world domination in order to assist the West in the struggle against communism.

But figures such as these are never central characters; they are always villains, who oppose the hero. And with the last two, as well as others of the same kind, we are leaving the detective story for the adventure novel. For the criminal as hero or central character, we must turn to other types, who are usually to be found, like the detective of the period, in the short story rather than the novel. There is, for example, the master of disguise: Grant Allen's (1848–99) Colonel Clay, so called 'because he appears to have an indiarubber face and he can mould it like clay in the hands of the potter', a man who can transform himself almost instantaneously from a Mexican seer to a Scottish parson (*An African Millionaire. Episodes in the Life of the Illustrious Colonel Clay*, 1897). Another example is Thomas W. Hanshew's (1857–1914) Hamilton Cleek, 'the Man of the Forty Faces', also an indiarubber-faced character, whose 'features seemed to writhe and knot and assume in as many moments a dozen different aspects'. Love brings about Cleek's downfall; captivated, he yearns to reform, and addresses a pathetic plea to the strangely named Superintendent Maverick Narkom of Scotland Yard: 'I'm tired of being Cleek the thief; Cleek, the burglar. Make me Cleek the detective, and let us work together, hand in hand, for a common cause and for the public good' (*The Man of the Forty Faces*, 1910; US title *Cleek, the Master Detective*).

Another common character of the period is the shyster, the crooked small operator. Arthur Morrison, who has already been mentioned earlier as the creator of Martin Hewitt, a detective contemporary of Sherlock Holmes, also wrote a number of stories about a less scrupulous but more interesting character, Dorrington, a con man and thief who on occasion works as a less than honest private detective (*The Dorrington Deed-Box*, 1897). A similar figure is Romney Pringle, ostensibly a literary agent, who earns a precarious living by swindling crooks out of their ill-gotten gains. He appears in a single contemporary collection, *The Adventures of Romney Pringle* (1902), though a number of other stories, originally published in *Cassell's Magazine* from 1903, were much later collected as *The Further Adventures of Romney Pringle* (1969). The interest taken in these stories by connoisseurs of detective fiction stems from the fact, noted earlier, that they were written, under the pseudonym Clifford Ashdown, by R. Austin Freeman, in collaboration with a friend, Dr John James Pitcairn, then the medical officer at Holloway prison, where Freeman also worked for a short time. They are, however, far inferior to Freeman's Thorndyke stories.

A more powerful figure, who really transcends this category, is Randolph Mason, the skilled, unscrupulous lawyer who appears in stories by Melville Davisson Post (*The Strange Schemes of Randolph Mason*, 1896). He is described as a 'mysterious legal misanthrope, having no sense of moral obligation, but learned in the law, who by virtue of the strange tilt in his mind is pleased to strive with the difficulties of his clients as though they were mere problems involving no matter of right or equity or common justice'. Post himself was a lawyer, and at times the stories are perhaps overburdened with legal argument; but they are intended as propaedeutic entertainment, with the aim of demonstrating how 'a skilful rogue could commit crimes in such a way as to render the law powerless to punish him'. Mason himself is a less successful creation than the same author's Uncle Abner, but the stories are interesting and original.

GENTLEMAN-BURGLARS AND ROBIN HOODS

The most popular criminal hero of this time, however, is the gentle-man-thief, a romantic figure whose descent runs back through the gallant highwayman to Robin Hood. E. W. Hornung (1866–1921) began the trend when he created the famous A. J. Raffles, Test crick-eter ('the finest slow bowler of his decade'), gentleman, and thief, whose rooms in Albany are hung with pre-Raphaelite etchings, and who eventually dies a hero's death during the Boer War (*The Amateur Cracksman*, 1899; also as *Raffles, the Amateur Cracksman*). Raffles's Watson is Bunny Manders, once his fag at school, who, though a rabbit at cricket and none too quick on the uptake, is supremely loyal. Hornung is a better writer than Conan Doyle, his brother-in-law; his plots are neat and entertaining; and he has a nice ear, too, for the monstrous pun: 'What on earth are you going to do with this?' asks Bunny, when he sees Raffles, about to enlist, with a bottle of ladies' hair-dye. 'Dye for my country', replies Raffles sweetly. Nevertheless, the stories fail to be as memorable as the Sherlock Holmes series; Raffles and Bunny do not have the mythic stature of Holmes and Watson, and it seems likely, too, that stories about a criminal, no matter how excellent they are in their own right, can never be as attractive as stories about a detective. On the other hand, Barry Perowne's (pseudonym of Philip Atkey, b. 1928) later imitations of Hornung are probably more successful than any of the manifold attempts to imitate Holmes (*Raffles after Dark*, 1933; revised US edition as *The Return of Raffles*, 1933).

Raffles was quickly followed by a host of similar characters, none of whom is worth dwelling on. The best is undoubtedly Barry Pain's (1864–1928) Constantine Dix, a lay preacher who is also a thief; he narrates his own exploits, which is unusual in this type of story. Pain writes well, with a nice touch of irony; but Dix is neither as glamorous nor as interesting as Raffles (*The Memoirs of Constantine Dix*, 1905). The novelist Arnold Bennett (1867–1931) also contributed a Raffles-like character in the person of Cecil Thorold, an extraordinarily rich and extraordinarily handsome young man, who commits crimes to right injustices (*The Loot of Cities. Being the Adventures of a Million-aire in Search of Joy*, 1905). William Le Queux (1864–1927), who wrote a vast number of books, mainly mystery, crime, and spy stories, who was reputed to have been employed by the British Secret Service, and who was the favourite novelist of both Queen Alexandra and the King of Italy, produced a collection of stories about Bindo di

Ferraris, a young Italian aristocrat and thief who travels round Europe in his six-litre Bentley—later a Mercedes—leaving a trail of empty jewel boxes behind him. The cars are by far the best thing in the stories, which are appropriately narrated by the count's chauffeur, George Ewart, an Englishman (*The Count's Chauffeur. Being the Confessions of George Ewart, Chauffeur to Count Bindo di Ferraris*, 1907). Maurice Leblanc (1864–1941) added a French version with the famous Arsène Lupin, who always leaves his card, inscribed 'Arsène Lupin: Gentleman-Burglar', at the scene of the crime. The stories in which he appears are often ingenious, but perhaps even less serious in intent than most others; their tone can be judged from the fact that in one story Lupin crosses swords with the famous English detective Holmlock Shears, whom he easily bests (*The Seven of Hearts. Together with other Exploits of Arsène Lupin*, 1908).

Two American examples complete the group: Frederick Anderson's (1877–1947) master thief, the infallible Godahl, who brings to crime the same inhumanly logical, scientific mind that Jacques Futrelle's Professor S. F. X. Van Dusen, the Thinking Machine, brings to detection (*Adventures of the Infallible Godahl*, 1914); and Jimmie Dale, a young New York club-man, who has three other identities: Grey Seal, the 'most puzzling, bewildering, delightful crook in the annals of crime', whose name comes from the fact that, like Lupin, he leaves his visiting-card, a lozenge-shaped grey seal behind whenever he commits a crime; Larry the Bat, a member of the New York underworld; and Smarlinghue, an unsuccessful artist. Dale, extremely popular for a long time, appears in stories by Frank L. Packard (1877–1942) (*The Adventures of Jimmie Dale*, 1917).

After the war the type was revived by Bruce Graeme (pseudonym of Graham Montague Jeffries, 1900–82) with *Blackshirt* (1925). His hero, Richard Verrell, is a well-known mystery writer by day, but by night a gentleman-thief who dresses completely in black and even wears a black mask, presumably in order to escape notice. The book and its successor (*The Return of Blackshirt* 1927) both sold in large quantities, and were followed by many more. The author later gave his hero a seventeenth-century French ancestor, Monsieur Blackshirt, and a son, who subsequently becomes Lord Blackshirt. The series was continued by the author's own son, Roderic Jeffries, who wrote some twenty Blackshirt novels under the pseudonym Roderic Graeme.

A few years later Leslie Charteris (b. 1907) gave the hero slightly different characteristics when, in *Meet the Tiger* (1928), he introduced the debonair figure of Simon Templar, otherwise known as 'The Saint', a contemporary Robin Hood whose visiting-card depicts a little stick figure wearing a halo. Though the police, in both Britain and America, regard him with the utmost suspicion, they are never able to pin a crime on him. Meanwhile he rights wrongs, succours the poor, and metes out his own brand of justice to 'the ungodly', as he terms criminals in general. He differs from his predecessors in that his own criminal activities are very much played down—indeed, they hardly exist; he is a gentleman-adventurer rather than a gentleman-thief. His author once allowed him to explain his own existence, his philosophy of life, in the following words, which give a fair idea of the flavour of the novels:

I'm mad enough to believe in romance. And I'm sick and tired of this age—tired of the miserable little mildewed things that people racked their brains about, and wrote books about, and called life. I wanted something more elementary and honest—battle, murder and sudden death, with plenty of good beer and damsels in distress and a complete callousness about blipping the ungodly over the beezer. It mayn't be life as we know it, but it ought to be.

The Saint books, which have been coming out regularly from 1928 to the present day, have been immensely popular, and deservedly so, for they are fast-moving, exciting, ingeniously plotted, and often very amusing. A very similar, but far less successful, figure is John Creasey's the Honourable Richard Rollison, known to police as 'The Toff', another handsome, romantic gentleman-adventurer (*Introducing the Toff*, 1938).

By the 1960s, however, the gentleman-adventurer had become an anachronistic figure, and he was replaced by a character who was his opposite in every respect, Richard Stark's (pseudonym of Donald E. Westlake, b. 1933) Parker. Parker—it is significant that we are never told his first name—is a professional criminal, not an amateur like Simon Templar. But he is not only that: he is a passionless, emotionless machine for committing crime, for whom the normal small courtesies of social intercourse are as alien as they would be to a creature from outer space, a man completely independent of the rest of mankind, utterly sufficient unto himself. The character was an interesting experiment, and works well in the first books of the series, which are as harsh and as powerful as Parker himself. Later, however, given a permanent girl-friend, he softened and began to show signs of being in love. The first of the series is *The Hunter* (1962; UK title *Point Blank*).

Chapter 6

CONCLUSION

'One last question, Holmes', I said as I rose. 'Surely there is no need of secrecy between you and me. What is the meaning of it all?'

(A. Conan Doyle, *The Hound of the Baskervilles*)

In the century and a half since Dupin first appeared in print, the detective story has changed very little in essence. It has, it is true, become more complex and possibly more sophisticated, and has branched out into new areas. But it has avoided all the vagaries of literary fashion, and the principles laid down in Poe's works are still as valid as they were then.

During this period the detective, too, has changed very little. The triumvirate of amateur, professional, and professional amateur, represented by Dupin, Lecoq, and Holmes, are still around, though both their respective importance and their roles have altered. The heyday of the absolute amateur, the man-about-town for whom detection was an agreeable hobby, was the period between the two world wars. The type has now vanished completely, and must be, surely, impossible to resurrect—other than through the medium of the pastiche or the historical detective story. The other type of amateur, however, the detective who becomes involved in the investigation of a crime through his or her profession, is on the increase; and this can only be welcomed, as long as the professional knowledge and expertise of the character are put to good use by the author and not merely allowed to lie fallow. We might hope to see, for example, more characters like Dr Alex Delaware, Jonathan Kellerman's Californian child psychologist. Computer crime is an area which has been relatively untouched, perhaps because it is difficult to think of a way to make it entertaining. But there would certainly seem to be an opening for the software specialist as detective—though the kind of book with this subject that one naturally envisages would probably be closer to the thriller or adventure story than the detective novel.

Although the private detective also flourished in the 1920s and 1930s, his greatest period was possibly that before the First World War. Since then the history of the character has been one of an imperceptibly gradual decline. Whether the trend is irreversible or not would seem to depend on whether the type can be made more realistic, can be portrayed as uneccentric and normal, performing the kind of task that usually falls to the lot of the private detective. As in the case of the amateur detective, the day of the eccentric, larger-than-life character seems to be past. A start in this new direction may have been made by the female detectives of P. D. James and Liza Cody.

The great days of the private eye, a later creation, were probably from the 1930s to the late 1950s. It is difficult now to see the type as one which is capable of regeneration, but it obstinately refuses to lie down and die. Yet most present-day private eyes are hardly distinguishable one from another, being differentiated only by the city in which they work and one or two personal idiosyncracies. If the genre is to continue, it would seem that an effort must be made to vary not only the character of the private eye, but also the format of the narrative—in particular, to get away from that endless succession of interviews linked by bridging passages which has been the method of this kind of novel since the earliest days. At the same time some authors, such as Robert B. Parker, appear to have seen the writing on the wall and, while preserving the same series character, have increased the action and violence in their books to such an extent as to turn them once again into thrillers rather than detective stories.

The policeman, rather strangely, did not become an important figure in the detective story until the 1920s, but since then his progress has been the antithesis of that of the amateur detective, with a continuous increase in interest and popularity. It is true that we could probably make do with fewer novels in which the harsh brutality of crime is sentimentally counterpointed with the cosy domesticity of the detective's home life; but there can be nothing much wrong with a genre which has recently known such disparate and successful characters as Chester Himes's Coffin Ed Johnson and Gravedigger Jones, K. C. Constantine's Mario Balzic, Reginald Hill's Dalziel and Pascoe, P. D. James's Adam Dalgliesh, James Melville's Japanese policeman Superintendent Otani, James McClure's South African detectives Tromp Kramer and Zondi, and William Marshall's Yellowthread Street force, Hong Kong's answer to the Keystone cops. Of course, the police, rather than the gifted amateur or the hired professional, are the natural investigators of crime, a fact which frees the author from the necessity of erecting structures on a base which is essentially implausible, even though it does constrain him or her to do some research into the way in which a specific police force is organized and operates. Unlike the other types, too, there seems to be a good deal of scope for development in the police novel; the possibilities offered by, for example, the police forces of other countries, the police procedural, and the historical policeman are far from exhausted.

No doubt the detective story is capable of springing as great a surprise on the historian as its plot does on the reader. Yet it seems likely that the future of the genre lies largely with two types of detective: the amateur with professional knowledge and the professional with professional knowledge, the policeman.

FURTHER READING

The titles below have been selected for their interest and readability. It follows that the choice very much reflects the author's personal taste, and that not all the writers discussed in the text necessarily find a place here. Works mentioned in the text are not usually repeated in this list.

MARGERY ALLINGHAM (Albert Campion)

Look to the Lady (1931, US title *The Gyrth Chalice Mystery*); *Police at the Funeral* (1931); *Death of a Ghost* (1934); *Flowers for the Judge* (1936, also in US as *Legacy in Blood*); *Dancers in Mourning* (1937, also in US as *Who Killed Chloe?*); *The Case of the Late Pig* (1937); *The Fashion in Shrouds* (1938); *The Tiger in the Smoke* (1952); *The Beckoning Lady* (1955, US title *The Estate of the Beckoning Lady*)

FRANK ARTHUR (Inspector Spearpoint)

Another Mystery in Suva (1956); *Murder in the Tropic Night* (1961); *The Throbbing Dark* (1963)

H. C. BAILEY (Reggie Fortune)

Mr Fortune's Practice (short stories, 1924); *Mr Fortune Objects* (short stories, 1935); *The Bishop's Crime* (1940)

JOSEPHINE BELL (Dr. David Wintringham)

Death at Half Term (1939, US title *Curtain Call for a Corpse*); *Death at the Medical Board* (1944)

E. C. BENTLEY (Philip Trent)

Trent's Own Case (1936); *Trent Intervenes* (short stories, 1938)

ANTHONY BERKELEY (Roger Sheringham)

The Wychford Poisoning Case (1926); *The Poisoned Chocolates Case* (1929); *Top Storey Murder* (1931, US title *Top Story Murder*)

NICHOLAS BLAKE (Nigel Strangeways)

Thou Shell of Death (1936); *There's Trouble Brewing* (1937); *The Smiler with the Knife* (1939); *Malice in Wonderland* (1940); *The Case of the Abominable Snowman* (1941, US title *The Corpse in the Snowman*); *Minute for Murder* (1947); *Head of a Traveller* (1949); *End of Chapter* (1957); *The Widow's Cruise* (1959); *The Worm of Death* (1961); *The Morning After Death* (1966)

ERNEST BRAMAH (Max Carrados)

The Eyes of Max Carrados (short stories, 1923); *Max Carrados Mysteries* (short stories, 1927)

CHRISTIANNA BRAND (Inspector Cockrill)

Green for Danger (1944)

LYNN BROCK (Colonel Gore)

Colonel Gore's Third Case: The Kink (1925); *The Mendip Mystery* (1929, US title *Murder at the Inn*); *Q. E. D.* (1930, US title *Murder on the Bridge*)

LEO BRUCE (Carolus Deene)

Dead for a Ducat (1956); *Furious Old Women* (1960); *Death in Albert Park* (1964); *Death at St Asprey's School* (1967)

MILES BURTON (Desmond Merrion)

Death in the Tunnel (1936, US title *Dark is the Tunnel*); *Murder M. D.* (1943, US title *Who Killed the Doctor?*); *Not a Leg to Stand On* (1945); *Early Morning Murder* (1945, US title *Accidents Do Happen*); *Situation Vacant* (1946)

JOANNA CANNAN (Inspector Guy Northeast)

Death at the Dog (1939)

JOANNA CANNAN (Inspector Ronald Price)

Body in the Beck (1952); *Long Shadows* (1955); *And Be a Villain* (1958)

GLYN CARR (Abercrombie Lewker)

A Corpse at Camp Two (1954); *Swing Away, Climber* (1959); *Death Finds a Foothold* (1961); *Lewker in Norway* (1963)

JOHN DICKSON CARR (Dr Gideon Fell)

The Mad Hatter Mystery (1933); *The Blind Barber* (1934); *The Eight of Swords* (1934); *The Case of the Constant Suicides* (1941); *The Emperor's Snuffbox* (1942)

RAYMOND CHANDLER (Philip Marlowe)

Farewell, My Lovely (1940); *The High Window* (1942); *The Lady in the Lake* (1943); *The Little Sister* (1949, also in US as *Marlowe*); *The Long Good-Bye* (1953); *Playback* (1958)

G. K. CHESTERTON (Father Brown)

The Wisdom of Father Brown (short stories, 1914); *The Incredulity of Father Brown* (short stories, 1926); *The Secret of Father Brown* (short stories, 1927); *The Scandal of Father Brown* (short stories, 1935)

AGATHA CHRISTIE (Hercule Poirot)

The Murder of Roger Ackroyd (1926); *Lord Edgware Dies* (1933, US title *Thirteen at Dinner*); *Murder on the Orient Express* (1934, US title *Murder on the Calais Coach*); *Death in the Clouds* (1935, US title *Death in the Air*); *The ABC Murders* (1936, US title *The Alphabet Murders*); *Cards on the Table* (1936); *Murder in Mesopotamia* (1936); *Death on the Nile* (1937); *Ten Little Niggers* (1939, US title *And Then There Were None*, also as *Ten Little Indians*); *One, Two, Buckle My Shoe* (1940, US title *The Patriotic Murders*, also in US as *An Overdose of Death*); *Evil under the Sun* (1941); *Five Little Pigs* (1942, US title *Murder in Retrospect*); *The Hollow* (1946, US title *Murder After Hours*); *Mrs McGinty's Dead* (1952); *Curtain: Hercule Poirot's Last Case* (1975)

AGATHA CHRISTIE (Miss Marple)

The Body in the Library (1942); *The Moving Finger* (1942); *A Murder is Announced* (1950); *They Do It with Mirrors* (1952, US title *Murder with Mirrors*); *4:50 from Paddington* (1957, US title *What Mrs McGillicuddy Saw!*, also in US as *Murder She Said*); *Nemesis* (1971); *Sleeping Murder* (1976)

V. C. CLINTON-BADDELEY (Dr R. V. Davie)

My Foe Outstretch'd Beneath the Tree (1968); *Only a Matter of Time* (1969); *No Case for the Police* (1970); *To Study a Long Silence* (1972)

LIZA CODY (Anna Lee)

Bad Company (1982); *Stalker* (1984); *Head Case* (1985); *Under Contract* (1986)

G. D. H. AND M. COLE (Superintendent Henry Wilson)

Poison in the Garden Suburb (1929); *End of an Ancient Mariner* (1933); *Murder at the Munition Works* (1940)

J. J. CONNINGTON (Sir Clinton Driffield)

The Case with Nine Solutions (1928); *Mystery at Lynden Sands* (1928); *Nemesis at Raynham Parva* (1929, US title *Grim Vengeance*); *The Sweepstake Murders* (1931); *The Ha-Ha Case* (1934, US title *The Brandon Case*)

J. J. CONNINGTON (Superintendent Ross)

The Two Tickets Puzzle (1930, US title *The Two Ticket Puzzle*)

K. C. CONSTANTINE (Mario Balzic)

The Man who Liked to Look at Himself (1973); *The Blank Page* (1974); *A Fix Like This* (1975); *The Man who Liked Slow Tomatoes* (1982); *Always a Body to Trade* (1983); *Upon Some Midnights Clear* (1985); *Joey's Case* (1988)

GEORGE HARMON COXE (Kent Murdock)
The Charred Witness (1942); *The Reluctant Heiress* (1965)

EDMUND CRISPIN (Gervase Fen)
Holy Disorders (1945); *The Moving Toyshop* (1946); *Swan Song* (1947, US title *Dead and Dumb*); *Love Lies Bleeding* (1948); *Buried for Pleasure* (1948); *Frequent Hearses* (1950, US title *Sudden Vengeance*); *The Long Divorce* (1951, US title *A Noose for Her*)

FREEMAN WILLS CROFTS (Inspector French)
The Sea Mystery (1928); *The Box Office Murders* (1929, US title *The Purple Sickle Murders*); *Sir John Magill's Last Journey* (1930); *Death on the Way* (1932, US title *Double Death*); *Crime at Guildford* (1935, US title *The Crime at Nornes*); *The Loss of the Jane Vosper* (1936); *Death of a Train* (1946)

AMANDA CROSS (Kate Fansler)
The James Joyce Murder (1967); *The Theban Mysteries* (1971); *The Question of Max* (1976); *Death in a Tenured Position* (1981, UK title *Death in the Faculty*)

GLYN DANIEL (Sir Richard Cherrington)
Welcome Death (1954)

COLIN DEXTER (Chief Inspector Morse)
Last Seen Wearing (1976); *Service of the Dead* (1979); *The Dead of Jericho* (1981); *The Riddle of the Third Mile* (1983)

PETER DICKINSON (Inspector Pibble)
A Pride of Heroes (1969, US title *The Old English Peep Show*); *The Seals* (1970, US title *The Sinful Stones*); *The Lizard in the Cup* (1972)

CARTER DICKSON (Sir Henry Merrivale)
Death in Five Boxes (1938); *The Judas Window* (1938, US title *The Crossbow Murder*); *Murder in the Submarine Zone* (1940, US title *Nine—and Death Makes Ten*, also in US as *Murder in the Atlantic*); *She Died a Lady* (1943); *Behind the Crimson Blind* (1952)

A. CONAN DOYLE (Sherlock Holmes)
The Sign of Four (1890); *The Adventures of Sherlock Holmes* (short stories, 1892); *The Memoirs of Sherlock Holmes* (short stories, 1894); *The Hound of the Baskervilles* (1902); *The Return of Sherlock Holmes* (short stories, 1905); *The Valley of Fear* (1914); *His Last Bow* (short stories, 1917); *The Case-Book of Sherlock Holmes* (short stories, 1927)

A. A. FAIR (Bertha Cool and Donald Lam)

Spill the Jackpot (1941); *Owls Don't Blink* (1942); *Crows Can't Count* (1946); *Traps Need Fresh Bait* (1967)

KATHARINE FARRER (Inspector Richard Ringwood)

The Cretan Counterfeit (1954)

ANTONIA FRASER (Jemima Shore)

The Wild Island (1978); *Cool Repentance* (1982); *Oxford Blood* (1985)

NICOLAS FREELING (Van der Valk)

Gun Before Butter (1963, US title *Question of Loyalty*); *Double-Barrel* (1964); *The King of the Rainy Country* (1966)

R. AUSTIN FREEMAN (Dr Thorndyke)

John Thorndyke's Cases (short stories, 1909; US title *Dr Thorndyke's Cases*); *The Eye of Osiris* (1911, US title *The Vanishing Man*); *The Mystery of 31, New Inn* (1912); *The Singing Bone* (short stories, 1912; US title *The Adventures of Dr Thorndyke*); *A Silent Witness* (1914); *The Cat's Eye* (1923); *Dr Thorndyke's Case-Book* (short stories, 1923; US title *The Blue Scarab*); *The Puzzle Lock* (short stories, 1925); *The D'Arblay Mystery* (1926); *A Certain Dr Thorndyke* (1927); *Mr Pottermack's Oversight* (1930); *Pontifex, Son and Thorndyke* (1931); *When Rogues Fall Out* (1932, US title *Dr Thorndyke's Discovery*); *The Penrose Mystery* (1936); *Felo De Se?* (1937, US title *Death at the Inn*)

ERLE STANLEY GARDNER (Perry Mason)

The Case of the Counterfeit Eye (1935); *The Case of the Stuttering Bishop* (1936); *The Case of the Substitute Face* (1938); *The Case of the Perjured Parrot* (1939); *The Case of the Crooked Candle* (1944); *The Case of the One-Eyed Witness* (1950); *The Case of the Green-Eyed Sister* (1953); *The Case of the Sun Bather's Diary* (1955); *The Case of the Amorous Aunt* (1963)

WILLIAM CAMPBELL GAULT (Brock Callahan)

Day of the Ram (1956); *The Convertible Hearse* (1957); *Vein of Violence* (1961)

MICHAEL GILBERT (Chief Inspector Hazlerigg)

They Never Looked Inside (1948, US title *He Didn't Mind Danger*); *The Doors Open* (1949); *Smallbone Deceased* (1950); *Death Has Deep Roots* (1951); *Fear to Tread* (1953)

JOSEPH HANSEN (Dave Brandstetter)

Death Claims (1973); *Troublemaker* (1975); *Skinflick* (1979); *Nightwork* (1984)

CYRIL HARE (Inspector Mallett)

Death is No Sportsman (1938); *Suicide Excepted* (1939)

CYRIL HARE (Francis Pettigrew)

With a Bare Bodkin (1946); *When the Wind Blows* (1949, US title *The Wind Blows Death*); *That Yew Tree's Shade* (1954, US title *Death Walks the Woods*); *He Should Have Died Hereafter* (1958, US title *Untimely Death*)

MACDONALD HASTINGS (Montague Cork)

Cork in Bottle (1953); *Cork and the Serpent* (1955); *Cork in the Doghouse* (1957)

GEORGETTE HEYER (Superintendent Hannasyde/Inspector Hemingway)

Behold, Here's Poison! (1936); *They Found Him Dead* (1937); *A Blunt Instrument* (1938); *Envious Casca* (1941); *Duplicate Death* (1951); *Detection Unlimited* (1953)

REGINALD HILL (Dalziel and Pascoe)

An Advancement of Learning (1971); *Ruling Passion* (1973); *A Pinch of Snuff* (1978); *Deadheads* (1984); *Under World* (1988)

CHESTER HIMES (Coffin Ed Johnson and Gravedigger Jones)

The Crazy Kill (1959); *The Real Cool Killers* (1959); *All Shot Up* (1960); *The Big Gold Dream* (1960); *Cotton Comes to Harlem* (1965); *The Heat's On* (1966, also as *Come Back, Charleston Blue*); *Blind Man with a Pistol* (1969, also as *Hot Day, Hot Night*)

ELSPETH HUXLEY (Superintendent Vachell)

Murder on Safari (1938); *Death of an Aryan* (1939, US title *The African Poison Murders*)

MICHAEL INNES (Inspector John Appleby)

Hamlet, Revenge! (1937); *The Secret Vanguard* (1940); *The Daffodil Affair* (1942); *A Private View* (1952, US title *One-Man Show*, also in US as *Murder Is an Art*); *Old Hall, New Hall* (1956, US title *A Question of Queens*); *The Long Farewell* (1958); *A Connoisseur's Case* (1962, US title *The Crabtree Affair*); *Appleby at Allington* (1968, US title *Death by Water*)

P. D. JAMES (Chief Inspector Adam Dalgliesh)

A Mind to Murder (1963); *Unnatural Causes* (1967); *Shroud for a Nightingale* (1971); *The Black Tower* (1975); *Death of an Expert Witness* (1977); *A Taste for Death* (1986)

P. D. JAMES (Cordelia Gray)

The Skull beneath the Skin (1982)

DAN KAVANAGH (Duffy)

Fiddle City (1981); *Putting the Boot In* (1985); *Going to the Dogs* (1987)

H. R. F. KEATING (Inspector Ghote)

Inspector Ghote's Good Crusade (1966); *Inspector Ghote Breaks an Egg* (1970); *Filmi, Filmi, Inspector Ghote* (1976); *The Body in the Billiard Room* (1987)

JONATHAN KELLERMAN (Alex Delaware)

Blood Test (1986); *Over the Edge* (1987)

C. H. B. KITCHIN (Malcolm Warren)

Crime at Christmas (1934); *Death of His Uncle* (1939); *The Cornish Fox* (1949)

RONALD KNOX (Miles Bredon)

The Footsteps at the Lock (1928); *The Body in the Silo* (1934, US title *Settled Out of Court*); *Still Dead* (1934)

EMMA LATHEN (John Putnam Thatcher)

Accounting For Murder (1964); *Murder Makes the Wheels Go Round* (1966); *Come to Dust* (1968); *Murder Without Icing* (1972); *Green Grow the Dollars* (1982)

JONATHAN LATIMER (Bill Crane)

Headed for a Hearse (1935); *The Lady in the Morgue* (1936); *The Dead Don't Care* (1938)

PETER LOVESEY (Sergeant Cribb)

The Detective Wore Silk Drawers (1971); *Abracadaver* (1972); *Swing, Swing Together* (1976)

ED MCBAIN (87th precinct)

The Mugger (1956); *The Pusher* (1956); *The Con Man* (1957); *Killer's Choice* (1958); *Lady Killer* (1958); *Give the Boys a Great Big Hand* (1960)

HELEN MCCLOY (Basil Willing)

Cue for Murder (1942); *Through a Glass, Darkly* (1949); *Alias Basil Willing* (1951)

JAMES MCCLURE (Lieutenant Tromp Kramer)

The Caterpillar Cop (1972); *The Gooseberry Fool* (1974); *Snake* (1975); *The Sunday Hangman* (1977); *The Artful Egg* (1984)

JOHN D. MACDONALD (Travis McGee)

Nightmare in Pink (1966); *Darker than Amber* (1968); *A Tan and Sandy Silence* (1972); *The Turquoise Lament* (1973); *The Dreadful Lemon Sky* (1975)

PHILIP MACDONALD (Colonel Gethryn)

The White Crow (1928); *The Link* (1930)

ROSS MACDONALD (Lew Archer)

The Ivory Grin (1952, also in US as *Marked for Murder*); *The Barbarous Coast* (1956); *The Galton Case* (1959); *The Zebra-Striped Hearse* (1962); *The Far Side of the Dollar* (1965); *The Underground Man* (1971); *Sleeping Beauty* (1973)

NGAIO MARSH (Chief Inspector Roderick Alleyn)

Enter a Murderer (1935); *Death in Ecstasy* (1936); *Artists in Crime* (1938); *Death in a White Tie* (1938); *Overture to Death* (1939); *Death at the Bar* (1940); *Surfeit of Lampreys* (1941, US title *Death of a Peer*); *Died in the Wool* (1945); *Final Curtain* (1947); *Swing, Brother, Swing* (1949, US title *A Wreath for Rivera*); *Opening Night* (1951, US title *Night at the Vulcan*); *Scales of Justice* (1955); *Singing in the Shrouds* (1958)

WILLIAM MARSHALL (Yellowthread Street)

Gelignite (1976); *The Hatchet Man* (1976); *Thin Air* (1977); *Sci Fi* (1981); *Perfect End* (1981); *War Machine* (1982); *The Far Away Man* (1984); *Roadshow* (1985)

A. E. W. MASON (Inspector Hanaud)

The House of the Arrow (1924); *The Prisoner in the Opal* (1928)

JAMES MELVILLE (Superintendent Tetsuo Otani)

The Chrysanthemum Chain (1980); *A Sort of Samurai* (1981); *The Ninth Netsuke* (1982); *Sayonara, Sweet Amaryllis* (1983); *Death of a Daimyo* (1984); *The Reluctant Ronin* (1988)

GLADYS MITCHELL (Dame Beatrice Lestrange Bradley)

The Saltmarsh Murders (1932); *Laurels Are Poison* (1942); *The Rising of the Moon* (1945); *Tom Brown's Body* (1949); *Watson's Choice* (1955); *Spotted Hemlock* (1958)

ELLERY QUEEN (Ellery Queen)

The French Powder Mystery (1930); *The Dutch Shoe Mystery* (1931); *The Greek Coffin Mystery* (1932); *The Egyptian Cross Mystery* (1932); *The American Gun Mystery* (1933, also in US as *Death at the Rodeo*); *The Siamese Twin Mystery* (1933); *The Chinese Orange Mystery* (1934); *The Spanish Cape Mystery* (1935)

RUTH RENDELL (Chief Inspector Wexford)

Wolf to the Slaughter (1967); *The Best Man to Die* (1969); *Some Lie and Some Die* (1973)

JOHN RHODE (Dr Priestley)

The House on Tollard Ridge (1929); *The Davidson Case* (1929, US title *Murder at Bratton Grange*); *Peril at Cranbury Hall* (1930); *The Claverton Mystery* (1933, US title *The Claverton Affair*); *The Motor Rally Mystery* (1933, US title *Dr Priestley Lays a Trap*); *Hendon's First Case* (1935); *Death in Harley Street* (1946); *The Lake House* (1946, US title *The Secret of the Lake House*); *The Two Graphs* (1950, US title *Double Identities*)

DOROTHY L. SAYERS (Lord Peter Wimsey)

Clouds of Witness (1926); *Unnatural Death* (1927, US title *The Dawson Pedigree*); *The Unpleasantness at the Bellona Club* (1928); *Strong Poison* (1930); *The Five Red Herrings* (1931, US title *Suspicious Characters*); *Have His Carcase* (1932); *Murder Must Advertise* (1933); *The Nine Tailors* (1934); *Gaudy Night* (1936); *Busman's Honeymoon* (1937)

GEORGES SIMENON (Commissaire Maigret)

Pietr-le-Letton (1931, translated as *The Strange Case of Peter the Lett*, 1933); *Maigret et son mort* (1948, translated as *Maigret's Special Murder*, 1964, also in US as *Maigret's Dead Man*, 1964); *Les vacances de Maigret* (1948, translated as *A Summer Holiday*, 1950, also in US as *No Vacation for Maigret*, 1953); *La première enquête de Maigret* (1949, translated as *Maigret's First Case*, 1958); *Maigret et la grande perche* (1951, translated as *Maigret and the Burglar's Wife*, 1955); *Maigret en meublé* (1951, translated as *Maigret Takes a Room*, 1960; also in US as *Maigret Rents a Room*, 1961); *Maigret se trompe* (1953, translated as *Maigret's Mistake*, 1954); *Maigret voyage* (1958, translated as *Maigret and the Millionaires*, 1974); *Maigret et le clochard* (1963, translated as *Maigret and the Dosser*, 1973, also in US as *Maigret and the Bum*, 1974); *Maigret se défend* (1964, translated as *Maigret on the Defensive*, 1966)

MAJ SJÖWALL AND PER WAHLÖÖ (Martin Beck)

The Man on the Balcony (1967, translated 1968); *The Laughing Policeman* (1968, translated 1970); *The Fire Engine that Disappeared* (1969, translated 1971); *The Locked Room* (1972, translated 1973)

REX STOUT (Nero Wolfe)

The Red Box (1937); *Too Many Cooks* (1938); *Some Buried Caesar* (1939, also in US as *The Red Bull*); *Over My Dead Body* (1940); *The Silent Speaker* (1946); *Too Many Women* (1947); *And Be a Villain* (1948, UK title *More Deaths than One*); *The Second Confession* (1949); *In the Best Families* (1950, UK title *Even in the Best Families*); *Murder by the Book* (1951); *Before Midnight* (1955); *If Death ever Slept* (1957); *Champagne for One* (1958); *Plot It Yourself* (1959, UK title *Murder in Style*); *Too Many Clients* (1960); *The Final Deduction* (1961); *Gambit* (1962); *A Right to Die* (1964); *Death of a Doxy* (1966); *A Family Affair* (1975)

W. STANLEY SYKES (Inspector Drury)

The Harness of Death (1932)

JOSEPHINE TEY (Inspector Alan Grant)

A Shilling for Candles (1936); *To Love and Be Wise* (1950); *The Daughter of Time* (1951); *The Singing Sands* (1952)

SIR BASIL THOMSON (Richardson)

Richardson Scores Again (1934, US title *Richardson's Second Case*); *Inspector Richardson, C.I.D.* (1934, US title *The Case of Naomi Clynes*)

ARTHUR UPFIELD (Inspector Napoleon Bonaparte)

The Bone is Pointed (1938); *The New Shoe* (1951); *The Man of Two Tribes* (1956); *The Will of the Tribe* (1962)

S. S. VAN DINE (Philo Vance)

The Canary Murder Case (1927); *The Greene Murder Case* (1928); *The Bishop Murder Case* (1929); *The Scarab Murder Case* (1930)

ROBERT H. VAN GULIK (Judge Dee)

The Chinese Bell Murders (1958); *The Chinese Gold Murders* (1959); *The Chinese Lake Murders* (1960); *The Chinese Nail Murders* (1961)

HENRY WADE (Inspector Poole)

No Friendly Drop (1931); *Constable, Guard Thyself!* (1934); *Bury Him Darkly* (1936); *Lonely Magdalen* (1940); *Too Soon to Die* (1953); *Gold Was Our Grave* (1954)

COLIN WATSON (Inspector Purbright)

Bump in the Night (1960); *Hopjoy Was Here* (1962); *Lonelyheart 4122* (1967); *Charity Ends at Home* (1968); *The Flaxborough Crab* (1969, US title *Just What the Doctor Ordered*); *Broomsticks over Flaxborough* (1972, US title *Kissing Covens*); *The Naked Nuns* (1975, US title *Six Nuns and a Shotgun*);

One Man's Meat (1977, US title *It Shouldn't Happen to a Dog*); *Blue Murder* (1979); *Plaster Sinners* (1980); *'Whatever's Been Going On At Mumblesby?'* (1982)

CLIFFORD WITTING (Inspector Charlton)

Measure for Murder (1941); *Subject: Murder* (1945); *Dead on Time* (1948); *A Bullet for Rhino* (1950)

BIBLIOGRAPHY

The works on detective fiction that have helped me most in preparing this book are two histories of the genre: Julian Symons, *Bloody Murder*, 2nd rev. edn (Harmondsworth, 1985) and R. F. Stewart, . . . *And Always a Detective. Chapters in the History of Detective Fiction* (London, 1980); and three reference works: John M. Reilly, *Twentieth-Century Crime and Mystery Writers*, 2nd edn (London 1985), Jacques Barzun and Wendell Hertig Taylor, *A Catalogue of Crime* (New York, 1971), and Chris Steinbrunner and Otto Penzler, *Encyclopedia of Mystery and Detection* (New York, 1976).

Other general works on the subject are as follows:

Auden, W. H., 'The Guilty Vicarage', in *The Dyer's Hand* (London, 1963).

Barnes, Melvyn, *Murder in Print. A Guide to Two Centuries of Crime Fiction* (London, 1986).

Benstock, Bernard (ed.), *Essays on Detective Fiction* (London, 1983).

Cassiday, Bruce (ed.), *The Roots of Detection. The Art of Deduction before Sherlock Holmes* (New York, 1983).

Cawelti, John G., *Adventure, Mystery and Romance* (Chicago, 1976).

Craig, Patricia, and Cadogan, Mary, *The Lady Investigates* (London, 1981).

Dutruch, Suzanne, *Les techniques et les thèmes du roman policier anglais (Auteurs féminins) 1920–1950* (Paris, 1985).

Grossvogel, David I., *Mystery and its Fictions. From Oedipus to Agatha Christie* (Baltimore, 1979).

Haycraft, Howard (ed.), *The Art of the Mystery Story* (New York, 1946).

—— *Murder for Pleasure. The Life and Times of the Detective Story*, 2nd, rev. edn (New York, 1951).

Keating, H. R. F. (ed.), *Whodunit? A Guide to Crime, Suspense and Spy Fiction* (London, 1982).

Knight, Stephen, *Form and Ideology in Crime Fiction* (London, 1980).

Lambert, Gavin, *The Dangerous Edge* (London, 1975).

Messac, Régis, *Le 'Detective Novel' et l'influence de la pensée scientifique* (Paris, 1929).

Murch, Alma, *The Development of the Detective Novel* (London, 1968).

Narcejac, Thomas, *Une machine à lire—le roman policier* (Paris, 1975).

Ousby, Ian, *Bloodhounds of Heaven: The Detective in English Fiction from Godwin to Doyle* (Cambridge, Mass., 1976).

Queen, Ellery, *Queen's Quorum. A History of the Detective-Crime Short Story as Revealed by the 125 Most Important Books Published in this Field, 1845–1967)* (New York, 1969).

Routley, Erik, *The Puritan Pleasures of the Detective Story* (London, 1972).

Scott, Sutherland, *Blood in Their Ink: The March of the Modern Mystery Novel* (New York, 1953).

Usborne, Richard, *Clubland Heroes* (London, 1974).

Watson, Colin, *Snobbery with Violence* (London, 1971).

Winks, Robin W. (ed.), *Detective Fiction. A Collection of Critical Essays* (Englewood Cliffs, N.J., 1980).

Winn, Dilys (ed.), *Murder Ink. The Mystery Reader's Companion* (New York, 1977).

INDEX

Note. The names of authors and other real persons are printed in bold type; those of detectives and other fictional characters in ordinary type. Where a detective and author share the same name (as with Ellery Queen), references to both are to be found under the author entry.

Collinson, Peter, 39
Colonel Gore's Second Case (Brock), 35
Colt, Thatcher (Abbot),97
Come Home and Be Killed (Melville, Jennie), 119
Concerning Peter Jackson and Others (Frankau), 71
Connington, J. J., 83–4, 87, 97–8
Constantine, K. C., 117–18, 133
Continental Op (Hammett), 39–40, 43
Cool, Bertha (Fair), 42
Cooper, Fenimore, 14, 107
Cooperman, Benny (Engel), 46
Cop Hater (McBain), 110
Copper, Basil, 45
Cork, Montague (Hastings), 30
Cork on the Water (Hastings), 30
'Corkscrew' (Hammett), 40
Corpse in Cold Storage (Kennedy), 36
Corti, Inspector Franco (Inchbald), 105
Cotterell, Martin (Trench), 53–4
Coulson, John Hubert Arthur, *see* Bonett, John and Emery
Counterfeit Murders, The (MacClure), 88
Count's Chauffeur, The. Being the Confessions of George Ewart, Chauffeur to Count Bindo di Ferraris (Le Queux), 130
Courtier, S. H., 105
Cover her Face (James), 96
Cox, Anthony Berkeley, *see* Berkeley, Anthony
Coxe, George Harmon, 28
Cracksman on Velvet (Selwyn), 126
Cramer, Inspector (Stout), 23, 37
Crane, Bill (Latimer), 41
Crane, Frances, 69
Creasey, John, 27, 95, 113, 131
Cribb, Sergeant (Lovesey), 126
Crichton, Tessa (Morice), 67
Crime and Punishment (Dostoevsky), 122
Crime at Black Dudley (Allingham), 61
Crimebusters, 38
Crime d'Orcival, Le (Gaboriau), 6
Crispin, Edmund, 53, 66, 121, 122
Croft-Cooke, Rupert, *see* Bruce, Leo
Crofts, Freeman Wills, 7, 82–3, 85, 107
Crook, Arthur (Gilbert, A.), 23–4
Crosby, Inspector (Beeding), 87
Cross, Amanda, 55
Crossen, Kendell, *see* Chaber, M. E.
Crow, Inspector John (Lewis, R.), 119
Cuff, Sergeant (Collins), 4, 5, 80

Cumberland, Marten, 103
Cummings, Detective Inspector (McGuire), 88
Cunning as a Fox (Halliday), 27
Cunningham, E. V., 100

D.A. Calls It Murder, The (Gardner), 23
Dain Curse, The (Hammett), 39, 40
Dale, Jimmie (Packard), 130
Dalgliesh, Chief Inspector Adam (James), 7, 96–7, 133
Daly, Carroll John, 38–9, 40
Daly, Elizabeth, 76–7
Dalziel, Superintendent Andrew (Hill), 120, 133
Dance of Death (McCloy), 27
Dane, Clemence, 66
Daniel, Glyn, 53
Daniels, Charmian (Melville, Jennie), 119
Dan Kearney Associates (Gores), 46
Dannay, Frederic, *see* Queen, Ellery
Dark Light, The (Spicer), 44
Dark Mirror, The (Copper), 45
Dark Road (Disney), 30
Dark Wind, The (Hillerman), 108
Davey, Jocelyn, 54–5
Davie, Dr R. V. (Clinton-Baddeley), 56
Daviot, Gordon, 92
Dax, Commissaire Saturnin (Cumberland), 103
Dead in a Row (Butler), 119
Dead in the Morning (Yorke), 56
Dead Lion (Bonett), 54
Dead Men Don't Ski (Moyes), 69
Dead of a Counterplot (Nash), 55
Dead on the Level, *see* *Gold Coast Nocturne*
Dead Reckoning (Bonnamy), 53
Dead Skip (Gores), 46
Dead Stop, *see* *Dark Road*
Dean, S. F. X., 56
Deane, Carolus (Bruce), 54
Death About Face, *see* *About Face*
Death and Taxes (Dodge), 31
Death and the Maiden (Radley), 121
Death and the Pregnant Virgin (Haymon), 121
Death at the Dam, *see* *Sabotage*
Death at the President's Lodgings (Innes), 94
Death at Three, *see* *Eight Faces at Three*
Death Before Breakfast, *see* *Sabotage*
Death for Dear Clara (Patrick), 95